Competence-Based
Assessment Techniques

The Kogan Page Practical Trainer Series

Series Editor: Roger Buckley

How to Take a Training Audit Michael Applegarth
A Practical Approach to Group Training David Leigh
Designing Competence-Based Training Shirley Fletcher
How to Write and Prepare Training Materials Nancy Stimson
Selecting and Using Training Aids David Flegg and Josephine McHale
How to Design and Deliver Induction Training Programmes Michael Meighan
One-to-One Training and Coaching Skills Roger Buckley and Jim Caple
The In-House Trainer as Consultant Mike Saunders and Keith Holdaway

PRACTICAL TRAINER SERIES

KOGAN PAGE

Competence-Based Assessment Techniques

SHIRLEY FLETCHER

KOGAN PAGE
Published in association with the
Institute of Training and Development

To Dad, who taught me how to spell

First published in 1992
Reprinted 1992, 1993, 1994

Kogan Page Limited
120 Pentonville Road
London N1 9JN

© Shirley Fletcher, 1992

371.3
FLE

British Library Cataloguing in Publication Data

A CIP record of this book is available from the British Library.

ISBN 0 7494 0441 8

Typeset by Koinonia Ltd, Bury
Printed and bound in Great Britain by
Biddles Ltd, Guildford and King's Lynn

Contents

Series Editor's Foreword *Roger Buckley*   6
Acknowledgements   8
Introduction   9

PART I FOUNDATIONS OF COMPETENCE-BASED ASSESSMENT   11

1 Different Competence-based Systems   **13**
   Summary   13
   Which Competence-based System?   14
   Starting on the Right Foot   18
   A Comparison of Assessment Principles and Practice   20

2 What is Competence-based Assessment?   **24**
   Summary   24
   All Forms of Assessment have a Common Factor   25
   The Purpose of Assessment   25
   The Assessment Process   26
   Competence-based Assessment   28
   Practical Implications of Competence-based Assessment   29

3 Purposes and Uses of Competence-based Assessment   **32**
   Summary   32
   Introduction   33
   Assessment for Certification   35
   Case study: Whitbread Beer Company   35
   Enhancing Standards   41
   Performance Appraisal   41
   Identification of Training Needs   43
   Skills Audit   44
   Accreditation of Prior Learning   45

Selection and Recruitment   45
Evaluating Training   46

PART II PRACTICAL APPLICATION   49

4 Setting Criteria for Required Performance   **51**
   Summary   51
   Why am I Assessing?   52
   What is to be Assessed?   53
   Establishing Criteria for Performance   53
   Using Standards of Competence   58
   Agreeing Assessment Plans   62
   Establishing an Assessment Plan   62
   Influences on Assessment   64

5 Collecting Evidence of Competence   **67**
   Summary   67
   Who Assesses?   68
   Case Study: British Telecom   69
   Sources of Evidence   72
   Choosing the Right Assessment Methods   75
   When and Where should Assessment Take Place?   78

6 Matching Evidence to Standards   **80**
   Summary   80
   Introduction   80
   Types of Evidence   81
   Methods and Quality   84
   Rules for Assessment Methods   85
   Rules of Evidence   86
   Matching Evidence and Judging Competence   88

7 Review and Follow-up   **93**
   Summary   93
   Identifying Training Needs   93
   Recording Evidence   94
   Recording Achievement   96
   Providing/Arranging follow-up training   96

8 Quality-assurance Issues   **98**
   Summary   98
   Introduction   98
   Selection of Assessors   99
   Training of Assessors   100

Monitoring of Assessors   100
Verification Frameworks: Roles and Responsibilities   102
Approval of Assessment Sites   103
Procedures for Certification   104

References and Further Reading   106

Series Editor's Foreword

Organizations get things done when people do their jobs effectively. To make this happen they need to be well trained. A number of people are likely to be involved in this training: identifying the needs of the organization and of the individual, selecting or designing appropriate training to meet those needs, delivering it and assessing how effective it was. It is not only 'professional' or full-time trainers who are involved in this process; personnel managers, line managers, supervisors and job holders are all likely to have a part to play.

This series has been written for all those who get involved with training in some way or another, whether they are senior personnel managers trying to link the goals of the organization with training needs or job holders who have been given responsibility for training newcomers. Therefore, the series is essentially a practical one which focuses on specific aspects of the training function. This is not to say that the theoretical underpinnings of the practical aspects of training are unimportant. Anyone seriously interested in training is strongly encouraged to look beyond 'what to do' and 'how to do it' and to delve into the areas of why things are done in a particular way.

The authors have been selected because they have considerable practical experience. All have shared, at some time, the same difficulties, frustrations and satisfactions of being involved in training and are now in a position to share with others some helpful and practical guidelines.

This book complements Shirley Fletcher's other book in the Practical Trainer Series – *Designing Competence-Based Training*. The key issue addressed in this volume is how we assess competence. All of us are likely to be familiar with the techniques used to test or assess learning ability or attainment as part of the more traditional training programme. However, assessment of competences is all about actual performance in the work role which involves the trainer in collecting evidence of competent performance from a variety of sources.

The techniques for gathering such evidence are of value to all trainers and in particular to those in organizations that are working towards national qualifications or which choose to base their training on competences.

ROGER BUCKLEY

Acknowledgements

The author would like to acknowledge and thank the following people for their help in preparing this book: the Project Team at Whitbread for the inclusion of the case study; Mike Saunders at British Telecom for the inclusion of the case study; Dave Stuart at Moorfoot for permission to use a range of examples from *Competence and Assessment*; and Della for her wizardry at wood processing the diagrams.

Introduction

There has been much confusion in the last few years regarding the 'competence movement'. The question of what we mean by competence has been compounded by a plethora of technical papers, government edicts and general guidance documents which refer to occupational competence and personal competence. The latest addition, 'general competence', does nothing to ease what is increasingly being seen as a bureaucratic maze.

Add to this the further confusion between different competence-based models used on both sides of the Atlantic and it is no wonder that employers, trainers, managers and researchers tend to wonder which way to turn next!

This is unfortunate, for competence-based systems have much to recommend them. The flexibility of such systems could provide a much needed boost to the training and education arena, to work performance as a whole and thus to the competitiveness of companies in world markets. This is especially true in the UK.

Competence-based systems operate with two different emphases. In the UK, the system focuses on 'standards of occupational performance'. In the USA, the emphasis has been on 'competency development'. Both systems are criticized for not providing an 'overall' package of competency descriptors and each system has its ardent supporters.

However, the national, technical and academic arguments detract from the key benefits that can be drawn from competence-based systems at organizational level, whether this be from use of one system or a synthesis of both. Similarly, those who continually attack the new systems are often those who also attack the traditional ones!

Traditional education and training systems and frameworks have themselves been criticized for many years. Employers complain that 'qualified' people – those who have completed a 'recognized' course of learning – only *know what to do;* they cannot *actually do it.* The costs of such programmes are also a bone of contention (and always will be while employers fail to see education and training as an investment).

With competence-based systems, we have, at last, the opportunity to introduce training and assessment which focus on *actual performance*. It also provides a framework in which *evaluation of training effectiveness*, as well as *assessment of individual performance* can operate. Employers have long been asking for a framework in which *measurement* of these important contributors to economic effectiveness can operate. We now have the foundation for this framework.

In this book, which complements my two previous volumes on competence-based systems (Fletcher 1991a, 1991b), the what, why, when, where, how and who of competence-based assessment are explored in detail. I draw from my own experience at national and organizational level to present a warts-and-all picture of the key principles, methods, components, implications and benefits of competence-based assessment. I also offer practical guidance for those readers who are considering the introduction of this form of assessment – whether that introduction is in connection with defined qualification systems or for other purposes.

Part I provides a foundation for those new to competence-based systems. It deals with three questions: What are the differences between competence-based systems? What is competence-based assessment? How can I use competence-based assessment in my organization? Part II provides practical help in introducing assessment, including training of assessors and the establishment of quality-assurance systems.

Part I FOUNDATIONS OF COMPETENCE-BASED ASSESSMENT

Part I provides a foundation on which to base the plan of your competence-based assessment system. It answers three questions:

- What are the differences between competence-based systems?
- What is competence-based assessment?
- How can I use competence-based assessment in my organization?

Chapter 1 provides examples of competence-based models and outlines the differences between them. It also provides a checklist to help you determine whether the system you are considering is really competence-based.

Chapter 2 outlines the basic principles, concepts and operational implications of competence-based assessment.

Chapter 3 helps you to decide on the uses to which competence-based assessment can be put within your organization.

1

Different Competence-based Systems

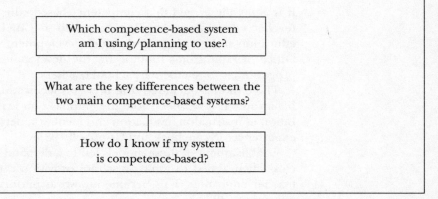

▷   S U M M A R Y   ◁

This chapter helps you to understand the foundations on which a competence-based assessment system operates. It also highlights the existence of two different competence-based systems and provides you with a general overview of each. Included in this chapter is a checklist to help you decide whether the system you are currently using (or planning to use) is really competence-based.

Which competence-based system
am I using/planning to use?

What are the key differences between the
two main competence-based systems?

How do I know if my system
is competence-based?

In the UK, competence-based systems are based on standards defined by industry. However, there is more than one competence-based system in existence. All are based on explicit behaviourial or outcome-based statements. In the UK, these statements are called 'criterion-referenced standards of occupational performance'. In the USA, they are 'criterion-validated'. This basically means that they relate to *real-life requirements of performance* and reflect *outputs* rather than *inputs*.

The format and basis of various systems varies because they are based on different concepts of competence. All competence-based systems are, however, based on research with *role holders*. In other words, the standards (or competences) which form the basis of a competence-based system of assessment are developed through research which involves the people who are actually doing the specific work roles.

The following section provides a brief outline of the development and use of the major competence-based assessment systems.

Which Competence-based System?

The competence-based movement has been in existence for some time. From the 1960s onwards, however, there has been an increasing demand in the business world, for greater accountability and more effective means of measuring and managing performance. This has led to research into what makes people effective and what constitutes a competent worker. Consequently, several different models of competence have emerged.

USA – Early Models

It is generally agreed that competence-based education has its roots in teacher education – usually referred to as CBET: competency based education and training – and that its development was fuelled by the US Office of Education's funding for the development of model training programmes for elementary school teachers.

These models included 'the precise specification of competences or behaviours *to be learned*, [note the emphasis on learning] the modularization of instruction, evaluation and feedback, personalization and field experience' (Swancheck and Campbell 1981).

Establishment of these models led to a demand for certification policies which aimed to improve school provision through the reform of teacher education. This became known as performance-based teacher education (PBTE).

As might be expected, the introduction of CBET in the USA caused a strong reaction from the higher education institutions, who perceived this new trend as a threat to their autonomy and academic status. A system of this kind also requires considerable reorganization of resources – an issue which affects the education and training arena at all levels.

CBET was, however, supported by the US Office of Education who promoted the new trend through the National Consortium of Competency-based Education Centers. This consortium established a set of 'criteria for describing and assessing competency-based programs'. (see Figure 1.1)

Competency specifications

1. Competences are based on an analysis of the professional role(s) and/or a theoretical formulation of professional responsibilities.
2. Competency statements describe outcomes expected from the performance of professionally related functions, or knowledge, skills and attitudes thought to be essential to the performance of those functions.
3. Competency statements facilitate criterion-referenced assessment.
4. Competences are treated as tentative predictors of professional effectiveness and are subjected to continual validation procedures.
5. Competences are specified and made public prior to instruction.
6. Learners completing the CBET programme demonstrate a wide range of competency profiles.

Assessment

13. Competency measures are validly related to competency statements.
14. Competency measures are specific, realistic and sensitive to nuance.
15. Competency measures discriminate on the basis of standards set for competency demonstration.
16. Data provided by competency measures are manageable and useful in decision-making.
17. Competency measures and standards are specified and made public prior to instruction.

Source: Bourke *et al.* 1975.

Figure 1.1 *CBET criteria for describing and assessing competence-based programmes*

The text also refers to criteria for 'instruction', for 'governance and management' and for the 'total programme'. The emphasis is on 'learning' and 'instruction' rather than assessment of actual workplace performance. This type of competence specification is most often used as part of a 'competence development programme'. It is essential to be clear, therefore, whether the key purpose of the competences is *development* or *assessment of performance.*

Difficulties arose in the USA because compliance with all the requirements within these stated criteria meant a complete review and reorganization of the education system.

This early model was focused on teacher training and very much centred in the educational forum. Plans to expand this to the vocational sector were hampered by the misunderstanding that the vocational system had always been competence-based! In fact, the US system, like that in the UK, was one in which curricula were devised centrally for institution-based education and often placed more emphasis on theory and knowledge than on practical application in the workplace.

Federal funding was made available to stimulate the use of competence-based systems in the vocational sector but the emphasis remained on PBTE.

Guidance on the development and use of competence-based systems of learning and assessment began to proliferate. A further model was proposed by Elam (1971) and has been used extensively to explain competence-based systems in respect of vocational education and training. It provides a useful starting point – but one word of warning: make no assumptions about the terminology! Recognition of the terms is no guarantee that 'we already do that'. The fact that many aspects of competence-based provision have been tacked on to existing curricula does not make the revised product competence-based! Notice again the use of the terms 'progress' 'learning' and 'programmes' in Figure 1.2.

Essential elements

1. Competences are role derived, specified in behaviourial terms and made public.
2. Assessment criteria are competence-based, specify mastery levels and are made public.
3. Assessment requires performance as prime evidence but takes knowledge into account.
4. Individual student progress rate depends on demonstrated competency.
5. The instructional programme facilitates development and evaluation of specific competences.

Implied characteristics

1. Individualization of learning.
2. Feedback to learners.
3. Emphasis on exit rather than admission requirements.
4. Systematic programme.
5. Modularization.
6. Student and programme accountability.

Related desirable characteristics

1. Field setting for learning.
2. Broad base for decision-making.
3. Provision of protocol and training materials.
4. Student participation in decision making.
5. Research oriented and regenerative.
6. Career continuous.
7. Role integration.

Source: Elam 1971

Figure 1.2 *Characteristics of Elam's early competence-based programmes*

USA – Hay McBer Models

A second widely used model is concerned with the identification of characteristics in superior performers of an occupational role. It is often referred to as the system which relates to 'soft skills'.

The work originates at the McBer Corporation and Harvard Business School. Competencies (note the difference in spelling from the UK 'competences') are derived through use of a form of critical incident analysis, using highly successful or 'excellent' performers as a research group. The resulting underlying characteristics, organized into 'clusters', have been used in management education and training in the USA and UK.

Competence here is defined in terms of the characteristics of individuals. Competence is something which is 'held' or 'owned' by the individual and brought to the occupational role.

Examples of the McBer competency clusters are illustrated in Figure 1.3.

Goal and action cluster deals with the manager's initiative, image, problem-solving skills and goal orientation.

- Efficiency orientation
- Proactivity
- Concern with impact
- Diagnostic use of concepts

Directing subordinates cluster involves a manager's freedom of expression both in terms of giving directives and orders, and giving feedback to help develop subordinates.

- Use of unilateral power
- Developing others
- Spontaneity

Human resource cluster Managers with these competencies have positive expectations about others, have realistic views of themselves, build networks or coalitions with others to accomplish tasks and stimulate cooperation and pride in work in groups.

- Accurate self-assessment
- Self-control
- Stamina and adaptability
- Perceptual objectivity
- Positive regard
- Managing group process
- Use of socialized power

Leadership cluster represents a manager's ability to discern the key issues, patterns or objectives in an organization, and to then conduct himself or herself and communicate in a strong fashion.

- Self-confidence
- Self-conceptualization
- Logical thought
- Use of oral presentations

Figure 1.3 *The competency programme of the American Management Association*

The UK Competency System

In the early 1970s, the New Training Initiative (MSC 1981) first launched the idea of 'standards of a new kind'. White Papers in 1986 and a review of vocational qualifications in the same year led to the beginning of the Standards Development Programme. The then Manpower Services Commission was charged with managing the development of occupational standards of performance for all sectors of all industries.

The review of vocational qualifications also led to the establishment of the National Council for Vocational Qualifications (NCVQ) which was to take responsibility for the development of criteria for a new framework of qualifications based on these new employment-led standards of competence.

A huge development programme began. 'Industry lead bodies' were established and charged with project-management responsibilities for standards development within their own sectors. The Standards Methodology Unit at the MSC (which had become the Training Agency) managed a wide range of projects to establish the methodology for the development of standards and associated assessment and certification systems.

The UK standards of occupational competence (see Figure 1.4) are different in format and in basic concept from those in the McBer system. They are also being developed for *all* occupational roles in *all* sectors of industry and commerce. In the UK, competence-based standards reflect the *expectations of workplace performance*. The establishment of 'personal competences' to supplement these occupationally related standards has been accomplished, but their use has yet to be fully tested.

Starting on the Right Foot

To say 'we are introducing competence-based assessment' is a very broad statement. If your organization is considering this development, and if you are charged with the initial research or with the implementation process, then consider the following before making any definitive decisions:

- Which system would best meet our needs?
- What are the implications of each?
- What are the key differences?
- What do we want to assess –
  – occupational competence?
  – personal competence?
  – general competence?
  – all three or any combination?

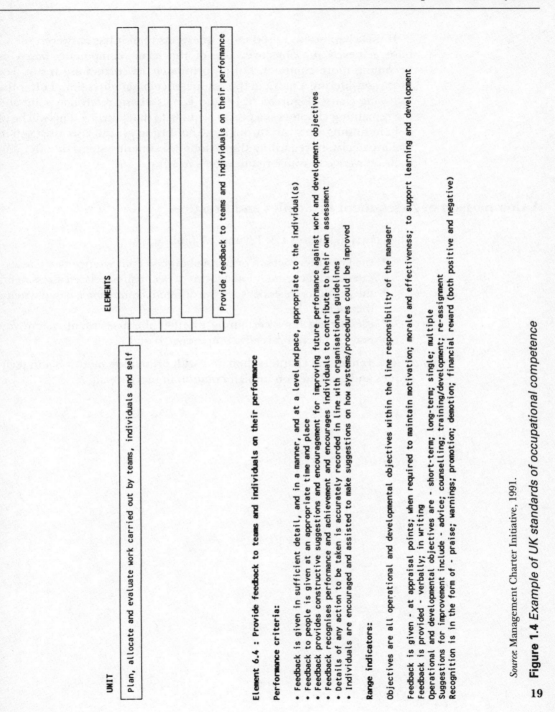

UNIT

Plan, allocate and evaluate work carried out by teams, individuals and self

ELEMENTS

Provide feedback to teams and individuals on their performance

Element 6.4 : Provide feedback to teams and individuals on their performance

Performance criteria:

• Feedback is given in sufficient detail, and in a manner, and at a level and pace, appropriate to the individual(s)
• Feedback to people is given at an appropriate time and place
• Feedback provides constructive suggestions and encouragement for improving future performance against work and development objectives
• Feedback recognises performance and achievement and encourages individuals to contribute to their own assessment
• Details of any action to be taken is accurately recorded in line with organisational guidelines
• Individuals are encouraged and assisted to make suggestions on how systems/procedures could be improved

Range indicators:

Objectives are all operational and developmental objectives within the line responsibility of the manager

Feedback is given - at appraisal points; when required to maintain motivation; morale and effectiveness; to support learning and development
Feedback is provided - verbally; in writing
Operational and developmental objectives are - short-term; long-term; single; multiple
Suggestions for improvement include - advice; counselling; training/development; re-assignment
Recognition is in the form of - praise; warnings; promotion; demotion; financial reward (both positive and negative)

Source: Management Charter Initiative, 1991.

Figure 1.4 *Example of UK standards of occupational competence*

If this chapter has raised more questions than it has answered then I have achieved my objective. Use of the term 'competence-based' is becoming more common, but unfortunately its correct use is not. For those considering a move in the competence-based direction, I offer the following charts (Figures 1.5, 1.6 and 1.7) as a basic reference point and the remaining chapters as a practical guide to that journey. This will be of help in finding your way through the confusion . It will also assist you in making decisions regarding the various assessment systems on offer and their relevance to your organization's needs.

A Comparison of Assessment Principles and Practice

The charts in Figures 1.5, 1.6 and 1.7 outline:

- the key differences in principle between competence-based assessment and more traditional forms of occupation-related assessment;
- the key differences between the different competence-based systems themselves;
- the criteria for ascertaining whether the assessment system you may be offered is really competence-based.

The remaining chapters then deal with principles, methods and techniques and guidance on implementation in more detail.

	Traditional	Competence-based
Concept	Assessment of learning ability or achievement	Assessment of actual performance in a work role
Foundation	Curricula, defined centrally by teaching staff/divisional boards	Explicit standards of required performance defined by industry (UK) or by research using 'excellent' performers (USA)
Assessment requirements	Assessment is an integral part of learning programmes	Assessment is independent of any learning programme
Evidence	Assessment evidence drawn from course assignments/exams	Assessment evidence collected from actual workplace performance supplemented by other methods
	Types of evidence predetermined by course syllabus	Types of evidence governed only by rules for quality of evidence
	Assessment is norm-referenced	Assessment is criterion-referenced (UK), criterion-validated (USA), and individualized

Figure 1.5 *Traditional vs competence-based assessment*

Criterion-referenced (UK)	Criterion-validated (USA)
Standards of performance (competences) developed and agreed by industry	Competency clusters developed by research using 'excellent' performers
Assessment of workplace performance	Learning and development of competence
Competence = expectations of employment	Competence = personal characteristics
Standards outcome-based (criterion-referenced)	Standards output-oriented (criterion-validated)
Standards of occupational competence (actual performance at work)	Educational process (competence development)
Sectorally agreed benchmark of competent performance	Specifications of 'superior' performance defined by educational research
Product – hard competences	Product – soft competencies

Figure 1.6 *Key differences between main types of competence-based assessment systems*

If you are considering the introduction of a competence-based assessment system and perhaps seeking advice from an external source, the following checklist will allow you to judge whether the proposals presented are truly competence-based.

Is the proposed system:
- based on the use of explicit statements of performance?
- focused on the assessment of *outputs* or *outcomes* of performance?
- independent of any specified learning programme?
- based on a requirement in which evidence of performance is collected from observation and questioning of actual performance as the main assessment method?
- one which provides *individualized* assessment?
- one which contains clear guidance to assessors regarding the quality of evidence to be collected?
- one which contains clear guidelines and procedures for quality assurance?

Figure 1.7 *Checklist for competence-based assessment .*

▶   REVIEW   ◀

This chapter has aimed to help you identify the key differences between two major competence-based systems and to clarify the key characteristics of each.

The guidance provided in this chapter will help you to decide which competence-based system is best for your particular needs. You need to keep in mind whether your system will aim to *develop* competence or to *assess competent performance.*

2 What is Competence-based Assessment?

▷   SUMMARY   ◁

This chapter helps you through the initial maze of competence-based assessment systems. It outlines the basic principles on which these systems operate. It also acts as a reference source for your decision-making.

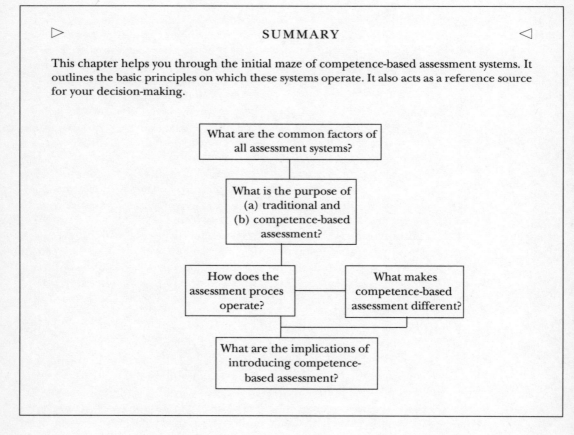

All Forms of Assessment Have a Common Factor

Assessment is about the *collection of evidence*. All forms of assessment can be included in this description – from everyday activities to the most complex statistical systems.

For example, when shopping for clothes you assess the suitability of various items by matching the qualities of those items to the set of *requirements* you have established for yourself. Your requirements may relate to price, size, colour, style and fit. You will therefore seek *evidence* from price tags and from examination and fitting of the items to help you make a judgement and final choice. Your final choice may allow for some compromise if you cannot find an item which meets *all* your requirements – that is, you will make a decision based on the best match of requirements and evidence.

Similarly, if you were taking a course of learning within a traditional vocational education and training system, you would be assessed by a tutor and/or examiner who would seek *evidence* that you had achieved the required *learning*. This evidence would be in the form of course assignments and probably a final examination, and would be matched against course *learning objectives*. The final decision would be influenced by a 'norm-referenced' process, in other words, your results will be compared with those of other people. You would need to achieve an agreed percentage in order to pass the assessment (or indeed gain a 'credit' or 'distinction').

There are many instances in which we are either assessing or being assessed. In each instance, the assessment concerns the *collection of evidence*. This is, therefore, the common factor within all forms and all types of assessment. So why are there so many types?

Although all forms of assessment concern the use of evidence, each form of assessment may have a different purpose. It is the *purpose* of assessment which will define the nature and process of the assessment system.

The Purpose of Assessment

The purpose of assessment when buying clothes is to collect sufficient evidence to enable you to buy the right clothes at the right price or the closest possible match between your requirements and what is available.

The purpose of assessment within a programme of learning is to collect sufficient evidence to demonstrate that you have *learned* at least the required minimum percentage of the syllabus. If the programme of learning is also linked to an award system, a further purpose may be the achievement of formal recognition that learning has been achieved. This usually takes the form of a certificate or diploma.

In a competence-based assessment system, the purpose of assessment is to collect sufficient evidence that individuals *can perform to the specified standards in a specific role*. If this assessment is also linked to an award system, a further purpose is formal recognition of successful performance.

The Assessment Process

A process is a 'series of actions or events', or a 'sequence of operations'. We could say that *all* forms of assessment involve the following sequence of operations:

- defining requirements or objectives of assessment;
- collecting evidence;
- matching evidence to requirements or objectives;
- making judgements based on this matching activity.

Our 'selecting clothes' assessment would follow the process shown in Figure 2.1, while the programme of learning assessment would follow that of Figure 2.2.

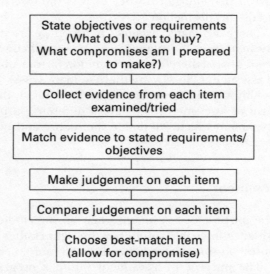

Figure 2.1 *Assessment process – selecting clothes*

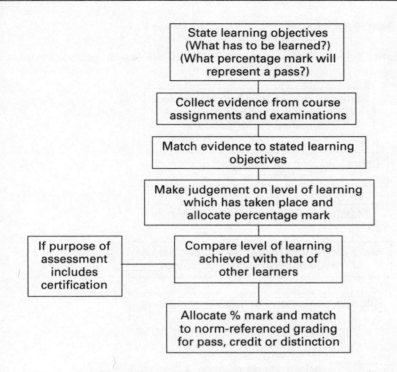

Figure 2.2 *Assessment process – programme of learning*

By comparing the two figures, we can begin to see how the purpose of assessment affects the assessment process and the assessment outcome.

In both examples the basic process of stating objectives, collecting and matching evidence and making a judgement is consistent with all forms of assessment as noted at the beginning of this section. However, at this point, different sequences of action are put into operation because the final *purpose* of assessment differs for each assessment event.

Both assessment events move along a *comparison* route. The first compares items assessed in order to make a *decision about the best item*. The second compares the results of the assessment with the results of other, similar assessments in order to *decide what final grading to apply*.

Both assessment processes follow a comparative approach – they both involve some form of comparison of assessment results. The second example involves 'norm-referencing', where an *average* achievement grade has been calculated and all *individual* achievements are judged against the average. Norm-referencing is the basis of most traditional assessment systems.

Competence-based Assessment

Figure 2.3 looks at the competence-based assessment process in the same way.

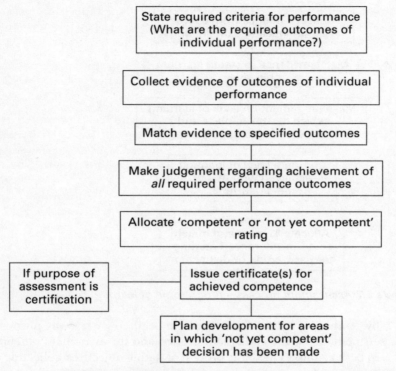

Figure 2.3 *Assessment process – competence-based assessment*

You may notice some key differences in the competence-based assessment approach:

- focus on 'outcomes';
- individualized assessment;
- no percentage rating;
- no comparison with other individuals' results;
- *all* standards (requirements) must be met;
- on-going process (leads to further development and assessment);
- only 'competent' or 'not yet competent' judgements made.

As we have already noted, the *purpose* of competence-based assessment is:

> To collect sufficient evidence to demonstrate that individuals can *perform* to the specified standards in a specified role.

We can add to this definition by clarifying that in competence-based assessment we are referring to *work roles* and therefore to *standards of occupational competence*. Occupational competence reflects *performance* at work. Our definition of the purpose of competence-based assessment will therefore look like this:

> To collect sufficient evidence of workplace performance to demonstrate that individuals can perform to the specified standards required within a specified occupational role.

This differs drastically from traditional forms of occupational assessment in which evidence collected relates to what has been *learned*. In competence-based assessment, our key concern is *actual performance*. Our focus is therefore, on *what individuals can do* rather than what individuals *know*.

This outlines the *key purpose* of competence-based assessment. The specific purposes or uses of this form of assessment are explored in more detail in Chapter 3.

Practical Implications of Competence-based Assessment

The introduction of competence-based assessment at national, organizational or departmental level has wide implications for managers, for trainers, and for those being assessed.

Unlike traditional forms of occupation-related assessment, competence-based assessment can be, and should be, undertaken *in the workplace*.

Who Assesses?

The first question then is if assessment is to be undertaken in the workplace, who are the assessors?

The most obvious choice is the supervisor or line manager. This arrangement raises a number of questions:

Do supervisors and managers have time to undertake formal assessment?

What if the supervisor or assessor doesn't like or has a poor relationship with the person being assessed?

What skills will assessors need?

What about Quality?

The second implication concerns the movement of assessment to a *local* rather than a *central* basis:

- How can quality of assessment be assured if it is undertaken locally by line managers?
- Who trains assessors?
- Who ensures that quality of assessment is maintained?
- Who pays for this?

How valuable is competence-based assessment?

In the UK, competence-based systems have been focused on the introduction of National Vocational Qualifications (NVQs). However, this really concentrates on only one use of competence-based assessment – assessment for certification.

We also need to consider what other purposes competence-based assessment can be put to within our organization, and what resources we will need.

What about training?

Last but not least is the issue of linking competence-based assessment to training. As the assessment system operates on a continuous – rather than one-off – basis, and is operated within the workplace environment, training needs are identified at individual level. Questions here include:

- What systems do we need to ensure that identified training needs are communicated to those who can take relevant action?
- In what way do we need to reorganize our training resources to provide training which meets those needs?

For educational institutions and for business organizations, the issues of resourcing, reorganization and administration are paramount.

All of these questions will be explored, together with possible solutions, in later chapters. For the present, it is important that you begin to think in terms of these issues.

▶ REVIEW ◀

This chapter has outlined the basic principles, purposes and objectives of assessment systems, particularly competence-based assessment. You should make sure you understand these basic principles before beginning work on your own scheme.

3 Purposes and Uses of Competence-based Assessment

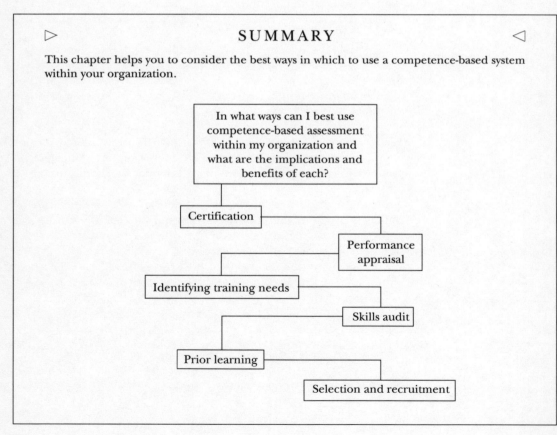

▷   **SUMMARY**   ◁

This chapter helps you to consider the best ways in which to use a competence-based system within your organization.

In what ways can I best use competence-based assessment within my organization and what are the implications and benefits of each?

Certification

Performance appraisal

Identifying training needs

Skills audit

Prior learning

Selection and recruitment

Introduction

Not all competence-based systems are based on standards defined by industry (as in the UK). They are, however, based on research with *role holders*. In other words, the standards (or competences) which form the basis of a competence-based system of assessment are developed through research which involves the people who are actually doing the specific work roles.

Obviously, you cannot use a competence-based system for any purpose until you have developed the competence measures. However, once you have the measures developed, they can be used for a whole range of assessment purposes.

One of the first considerations to be given to the introduction of any assessment system is *What is it we want to assess?* This may sound like a silly question, but it is one that is rarely addressed directly because assessment is often based on *assumptions* rather than clear and precise initial planning.

What do *you* want to assess? Are you planning to assess ability to learn (predictive assessment)? Are you planning to assess progress within a development programme (formative assessment)? Are you planning to assess performance (summative assessment)? Are you planning to assess at individual or group level?

Your next question must then be *Why are we assessing?* Is it to find out information about performance which is not currently available? Is it as part of a performance appraisal system? Is it to take a skills audit? Is it for manpower planning or selection and recruitment or the establishment of project teams?

Eventually, you will end up with the question *What measures are we using?* This is probably the most important question of all, although it cannot be dealt with in isolation from the others. Assessment concerns measurement – you must therefore know *what* you are measuring, *why* you are measuring it and *what form* of measurement will be used. Only when these questions have been answered can you consider issues of quality of assessment.

This chapter looks at the 'why' of competence-based assessment. It also builds on the previous chapter, from which you will recall that the key purpose of competence-based assessment is:

> To collect sufficient evidence of workplace performance to demonstrate that individuals can perform to the specified standards required within a specified occupational role.

In this chapter, we review the more specific purposes of competence-based assessment, and also continue to detail the key principles, implications and benefits which underlie this new trend. The following sections deal with each specific purpose in turn.

The traditional view

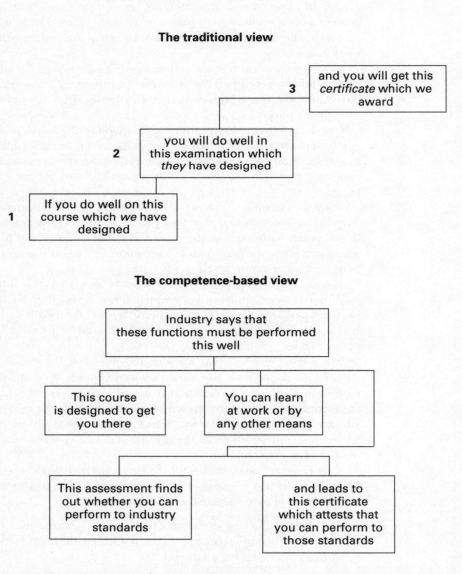

The competence-based view

Figure 3.1 *Key differences between traditional and competence-based approaches*

Assessment for Certification

In a competence-based system, assessment leading to certification refers to 'certification of competent performance', not to certification of ability to learn or to completion of a learning programme.

Think this through carefully. There is a huge difference between the various purposes of certification: consider some of the certificates you have seen at various times. What do these certificates actually tell you about the certificate holder? That the certificate holder:

- has *attended* a course of study or learning?
- has *completed* a course of study or learning?
- has demonstrated the *ability to learn to a particular level?*
- has demonstrated that specified theories/facts *have been learned?*
- has achieved a specified percentage grade in a *written* exam?
- has achieved a specified percentage grade in a *practical* test?

In a competence-based assessment and certification system, individuals achieve a certificate when they can *demonstrate performance which meets all the required standards*. Remember, there is no percentage grading, no norm-referencing, no pass or fail – only competent or not yet competent.

Figure 3.1 illustrates these differences between the traditional and competence-based systems.

National Vocational Qualifications (NVQs) are not the only form of certification which can be provided by competence-based assessment. Organizations may, for instance, wish to offer their own certification. National awarding bodies are flexible in their approach to such developments and will also offer joint certification of such systems. One example of this approach is the development of a company scheme at Whitbread Beer Company

Case Study: Whitbread Beer Company Cellar Service Division*

As competence-based standards and National Vocational Qualifications (NVQs) are being introduced across all sectors of industry and commerce, several key issues and implications for employers are emerging. Criticisms of the new developments often revolve around the following:

- the apparent high level of bureaucracy involved in implementation;
- the apparent incompatibility of the unit structure of NVQs with actual work roles;

*Adapted from an article prepared for *Education and Training*, August 1991.

- the relevance of a 'national benchmark of competence' at the organizational level.

One organization which acknowledged and acted upon this situation is Whitbread plc. The cellar service function, which consists of approximately 500 staff, developed a strategic approach to the improvement and recognition of their workforce. In a highly competitive market, Whitbread wished to prioritize staff development and the establishment of a high-quality training and assessment scheme to measure and manage individual and organizational performance and therefore provide a centre of excellence within the Whitbread operation.

Whitbread's action plan had several components:

- the definition and development of performance standards for all roles within the cellar service function (to incorporate the company mission statement and objectives);
- the design and implementation of an assessment process and quality-assurance system which would meet both operational needs and national criteria;
- the selection and recruitment of two training technicians who would design and deliver modular training based upon the new standards of performance;
- the training of all cellar service managers in competence-based assessment;
- agreement with a national awarding body for certification of competence against defined standards with links to the NVQ system.

Standards of performance were developed for each occupational role within the cellar service function and *by those who worked within those roles*.

Development work was undertaken alongside that for the introduction of BS5750 accreditation. The use of competence-based standards as a basis of quality in performance was found to be complementary to the use of BS5750 as a basis for quality of procedures.

The standards of performance will be used as a basis for the design of modular training programmes. Two training technicians were recruited and trained in the design of competence-based training. They also received extensive training in the operation of the in-house competence-based assessment system, thus enabling them to take over a key supportive role once the developmental project was completed.

In addition to their use as a basis for training and work-place assessment, the standards form a sound basis for recruitment and selection and for performance appraisal systems. They also form the foundation on which national certification of performance is based.

The Problem with Assessment and Certification

Introducing competence-based assessment can attract criticism from employers. Within a competence-based system or, more specifically, within the NVQ system, assessment leads to certification by a nationally recognized body. This national certification process requires that a quality-control mechanism is put in place – and it is in this respect that complaints about an over-emphasis on 'bureaucracy' are most loudly voiced.

It is also at this point that issues relating to the unit structure of NVQs are raised. If the main purpose of assessment is certification, and certification takes place on a unit-by-unit and 'whole qualification' (NVQ) basis, then employers are interested to ensure that their employees have access to a full NVQ.

This has presented difficulties. For some companies, the organization or content of work roles means that employees are able to obtain only some of the units required for a full NVQ; they feel that their employees should (or will want to) have access to the full qualification.

Once again, there appears to be a communication block on this point. NVQs are achievable on an individual basis, unlike traditional qualifications which are 'course-led' and achievable on the completion of a set period of study. Individuals can therefore build up their 'record of achievement' one unit at a time. Units may be relevant to more than one sector of industry. It is not, therefore, essential that everyone in every work role should be able to achieve a full NVQ while working in that role. The flexibility of the unit-based system means that individuals can obtain units which are relevant to their current and developmental roles, thus aiding their progression and helping employers to plan training, development and promotional operations.

This issue was addressed directly within the Whitbread cellar service project. Standards of performance had been prepared on a unit basis. However, the combination of units achieved by each individual employee could vary, and would also include units which reflected activities they undertook as part of their own development process. This flexibility is a key component of the Whitbread system, both from the employer and employee perspective.

Operationalizing Assessment

Once final standards had been agreed, the development and implementation of an in-house assessment system was undertaken. It was essential that the assessment system met five criteria:

- It must operate as a system for workplace assessment, building on managers' roles as developers of staff.
- It must operate as a common system across all occupational roles.
- It must be cost-effective in operation.
- It must operate as part of an effective quality-assurance system.
- It must meet national criteria and allow for certification by a national awarding body.

Documentation for recording assessment was designed to be user-friendly and to provide information required by a national awarding body. All line managers were trained by an outside consultancy in principles and operation of the competence-based assessment system. Internal verifiers – managers who would monitor and countersign the in-house system – were identified and trained with assessors. All assessors and verifiers were provided with their own copies of the consultancy's assessor guidance package, and arrangements to review their progress as workplace assessors were put in place.

To complement the system, and to continue the sense of involvement and ownership which had been generated by the development process, an individual development plan (IDP) was designed by the consultancy. Each individual was provided with an IDP which contained general guidance, the relevant performance standards, assessment documentation, a training record, and a section for storage of certificates obtained.

The line manager's role as an assessor includes the establishment of an assessment plan with each individual – the plan being recorded in the IDP. On-going assessment of normal workplace performance, with regular feedback, is then conducted and evidence of performance recorded on the assessment documentation. This system allows for training needs to be clearly identified and recorded on the training plan.

Identification of Training Needs

Using the Whitbread system, training needs analysis is undertaken by line managers and at individual level. Procedures for reporting training needs through the management structure were put in place and the development of modular training programmes begun. Once again, the flexibility of the system becomes clear – working at individual level allows for increased effectiveness in targeting of training delivery. Employees no longer have to attend a full training course in order to obtain perhaps 25 per cent of needed learning and development: the modular structure facilitates a focused approach to training and development needs.

The use of the individual development plan also links directly to BS5750 requirements. Each individual has a regularly updated record of training needs identified and action taken to meet those needs. Line managers keep copies of this training plan, and the assessment records.

Quality Assurance

Workplace assessors (line managers) are encouraged to establish support networks. At Whitbread, the managers plan to use time at regular meetings to discuss and exchange information regarding the assessment system.

Internal verifiers also provide line management support. Their role includes the countersigning of assessment records, sampling of evidence of performance and liaison with the awarding body external verifier.

As part of the quality-assurance model, an external verifier from City and Guilds will visit the company to monitor the assessment process. The system is completely open: external verifiers have access to all staff involved and can sample evidence of performance on an ad hoc basis.

With the standards and assessment system in place, each individual will be assessed and training needs identified. A three-year training plan is beginning with modular training focused on clearly identified needs.

The Timescale

Work began on the development of standards in December 1990. By March 1991, final standards for all occupations had been agreed, and the assessment system and quality-assurance mechanisms had been designed and agreed. Assessors were trained during April and May when agreements with City and Guilds were finalized. The assessment system then became fully operational.

The Outcome

Whitbread's cellar service now has an operational system which provides:

- performance standards linked to mission and objectives;
- one assessment system across all occupations;
- national recognition (including links into the NVQ system) for employee performance;
- the basis on which to identify training needs at individual level;
- training for all line managers in workplace assessment;
- assessment towards national certification as assessors for all line managers;
- standards as the basis of recruitment, selection and performance appraisal.

Enhancing Standards

Organizations may also wish to 'enhance' the standards on which qualifications are based in order to add in the company mission statement and objectives. If this is done in respect of NVQs, it is likely that you will need consultancy support for the development and early implementation stages.

Implications and Benefits

If you are considering the introduction of competence-based assessment for certification purposes you must first consider the following questions:

- What are we aiming to assess?
- Why are we assessing?
- What form of certification do we wish to provide?

If you take the nationally recognized qualification route, then you also need to consider issues relating to national quality criteria. For example, in the UK, NVQs are often awarded jointly by a recognized national body and the Industry Lead Body. Requirements for training of assessors, approval of assessors and assessment documentation may vary.

If you are considering a company qualification, then you will need to plan for resources to administer the system and to produce the certificates. Further help on this issue is provided in Chapter 8.

Joint certification with a national awarding body gives your workforce national recognition. You will need to negotiate with relevant bodies during and after the development of competency measures. Again, you may need consultancy support in this activity.

The certification issue is dealt with in more detail in Chapter 8 which focuses on quality-assurance issues.

Performance Appraisal

Many organizations have performance-appraisal systems. These usually operate on an annual basis and involve an interview with a line manager and use of a pre-interview question sheet.

Most criticisms of this system stem from the use of measures which are very difficult to assess and of rating scales which generally lead to assessors taking the 'middle road' as an easy option.

Competence-based assessment as the basis of performance appraisal provides a more specific measure of performance. However, in order to introduce such a system you must first define the competency measures to be used.

This can be done using a range of methodologies from functional analysis to DACUM to critical incident analysis to repertory grids. The important aspect to keep in mind is that competence-based systems use measures which reflect *outcomes*.

For example, DACUM ('developing a curriculum'), which involves using a group of experts to define their job role tends to focus on the *tasks* which individuals undertake within a specific *job*. Competence-based standards should focus on *functions* that are undertaken within an *occupational role*. This is because competence-based standards reflect a complete picture of a competent individual in a working context. This includes the tasks that the individual undertakes, and the way in which the individual organizes work to achieve those tasks and dealing with contingencies. It is therefore a rounded view of competence that should be portrayed in the defined standards.

Any analysis technique which focuses on *tasks* or on '*problem-solving*' approaches (such as critical incident analysis) should therefore be used with caution, and preferably used in conjunction with functional analysis, which operates from a 'top-down' perspective, beginning with the key purpose or mission statement of the sector or corporate body.

Many performance-appraisal (and other forms of) assessments use measures which are based on *inputs* (what has to be learned – see Chapter 1), or on *process* (the way in which work is conducted). Most trainers and many consultants find it difficult to shift their thinking to the degree required to develop *outcome-based statements*.

Implications and Benefits

A performance-appraisal system based on real measures of competence will provide an effective monitor of individual performance. However, before introducing such a system, consider the following questions:

- How we will develop the measures of competence?
- Who will develop them?
- How will success at performance appraisal link with career progression/pay/incentives?

In addition, competence-based systems provide the following added value but with associated development/implementation costs:

- competence-based assessment is continuous (formative) – this implies that assessment is not a one-off annual process;
- individuals have access to the measures of competence so that they know what is expected of them. What will be their attitude to this? Will they welcome involvement in their own development process?

There is also the question of what training managers will require.

Identification of Training Needs

Competence-based assessment offers an opportunity, through continuous measuring and managing of performance, for managers to identify training needs at individual level.

If such a system is introduced at organization level, the ability to identify these needs, and thus to provide training which is targeted to specific needs, is greatly improved.

Implications and Benefits

Operation of a competence-based system for the identification of training needs requires that managers are skilled in identifying real, rather than perceived, needs, in providing feedback, and in identifying those needs which can be dealt with by on-job development. A further added-value aspect of competence-based systems therefore is that managers are encouraged to take more of a development role. However, managers will need appropriate skills to achieve this effectively. Key questions in this context are:

- What training will our managers need in
    - identifying training needs?
    - coaching?
    - mentoring?
    - opportunity training?
- What communication structure needs to be in place to ensure that training needs are collated?
- What changes do we need to make to our training delivery function to provide modular development programmes?

This last question is often missed. If needs are identified more accurately, there is no longer a need for individuals to attend a 'standard' course – they need only attend courses where on-job development is not available or appropriate, and the course is modular in format and targeted to their specific needs.

At strategic level, identification of training needs as part of a skills audit, using a competence-based system, can assist with the development of corporate training strategies and plans, or indeed with manpower planning activities.

Skills Audit

All organizations would probably find it valuable to be able to take stock of their workforce skills. A competence-based system of assessment allows for this to take place either as an initial, introductory process (see also APL, p. 45) or as the result of collated data from an on-going assessment process.

You may consider introducing a computerized assessment recording system (keeping the Data Protection Act in mind of course). This is particularly useful in organizations which need to put together project teams, each member having specialist skills or expertise.

As an initial assessment, the competency measures can be used to assess current levels of performance (and identify training needs). As continuous assessment, the competence-based system allows for regular monitoring and updating of workforce skill levels.

For example, by providing individuals and their line managers with a copy of the standards which are relevant to their work role, and with guidance on their use, initial assessment will provide an analysis of current skills levels and training needs. As the assessment requires that evidence of competent performance is provided, and this evidence is generated from normal workplace activity, the individual can prove competence through the provision of relevant evidence.

Similarly, in a continuous assessment process, the level of competent performance, and training needs, continue to be identified.

In essence, a competence-based assessment system should make explicit what effective line managers do on a daily basis – *measure and manage performance*. Competence-based assessment should become an integral part of everyday management activity and involve line managers and those being assessed in a continuous process of development and improvement.

Implications and Benefits

Again, the measures must be in place before you start, so you may need to invest in this development. The use of accreditation of prior learning (APL) has its own implications and is dealt with in the next section.

The term 'skills audit' has unfortunate connotations. Any introduction in a strong union environment may therefore need careful planning and negotiation. The purpose of the skills audit must be clear if it is to be used as a positive motivator for improvement of performance.

Accreditation of Prior Learning (APL)

The APL process provides a useful tool in three areas:

- introducing competence-based assessment;
- taking a skills audit;
- as a staff development process.

APL is an integral part of competency-based assessment, not a separate process. It is one which allows for evidence from past achievements to be included in the total of evidence collected during assessment. There are particular rules of evidence (see Chapter 6) which apply in this context, but there is no reason why APL cannot be as reliable and effective as continuous assessment of performance – as long as quality rules are applied.

Implications and Benefits

APL is a useful tool for motivating staff and for introducing competence-based assessment. It requires trained assessors and probably advisers. It can be a very cost-effective process for skills audit. Check carefully about costs-per-head quotations when seeking advice from external sources. In my own in-company work on this issue, I have discovered that employers have been given wildly varying estimates of cost, particularly where APL is used in connection with assessment for certification purposes. In general, check for assessors approved by relevant awarding bodies if certification is one of your objectives. (Chapters 5–8 provide guidance for those of you who are considering the introduction of APL for certification or internal skills audit purposes.)

Selection and Recruitment

Again, the issue of having measures developed arises: you cannot assess competence unless you have a clear measure of competence to begin with. However, as noted in the introduction to this chapter, once you have the measures they can be used for a wide range of purposes.

Competence-based measures of performance focus on *outcomes*. If you know what outcomes you require, you can design your recruitment and selection processes around them.

Using the competence measures as a starting point, your recruitment material and interview schedules can be designed to elicit information which directly relates to required performance. (Note the use of the term 'schedules' for interviews – the implication is that questions are pre-determined and follow an agreed format and presentation. This will enable interviews to be conducted in a fair and effective way.)

Implications and Benefits

Recruitment and selection processes can be defined with more clarity using a competence-based system. The standards used as a basis for the design of these processes are common across all activities within the organization; there is therefore less chance of a mismatch between staff recruited and staff required. To implement such a system, time must be devoted to the development of interview schedules and training of interviewers. (Again, use of competence-based assessment leads to identification of training needs and requires that training is more systematic and directed to real needs.)

Evaluating Training

This is an area which has caused considerable concern but least remedial effort in many organizations. My personal belief is that as long as employers see training as a cost rather than an investment, little action will be taken to evaluate the effectiveness of training programmes. When training becomes an investment issue, the question of gaining the best possible return on that investment becomes important.

With competence-based assessment systems, the measures of competent performance are available for a before-and-after picture to be taken. If measures are used, as they should be, on a continuous basis to measure and manage performance and to identify training needs, then the measurement required to check on the effectiveness of training is already in place.

Training is too often an activity in which individuals are allocated to programmes on a 'grade-related' basis, or are sent to the most appropriate programme on the company's 'menu'. Far too few training consultancies actually make training applicable to the working context. So-called evaluation of programmes is in practice often no more than an enquiry as to the food, accommodation and whether participants liked the trainer.

If your organization needs to evaluate the effectiveness of training – and perhaps the effectiveness of managers' identification of *real* training needs – then a competence-based assessment system provides a framework in which this can be operated.

Implications and Benefits

Personally, I believe the 'return on investment' issue is a key one in this context. To establish competence-based assessment as a tool for training evaluation alone would be a costly exercise – but it is unlikely that this would be the case.

The key costs are in development – development of the competence measures and the associated assessment framework. Operational costs are minimal. Once competence measures are established they are available for use in the full range of business activities which have been outlined in this chapter. In effect, their use for training evaluation is a spin-off or added-value aspect of the implementation process.

> ▶ **REVIEW** ◀
>
> This chapter has briefly outlined the various purposes of competence-based assessment at organizational level. It also makes the key point that once measures are defined (or incorporated as nationally defined standards in the UK), they are available for use in the full range of assessment activities. Further guidance on the many issues, implications and benefits raised in this chapter can be found in the remaining chapters and in the References and Further Reading section.

Part II **PRACTICAL APPLICATION**

In Part II, you will be taken step by step through the process of competence-based assessment.

You may recall from Chapter 2, that our framework of competence-based assessment looked like this:

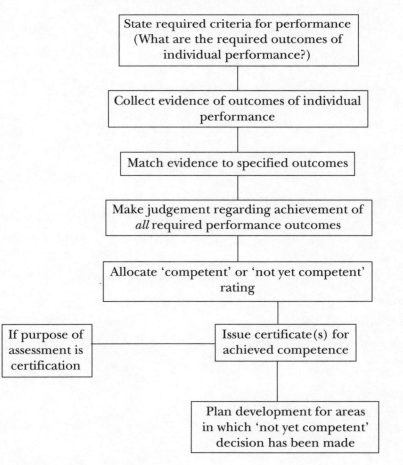

State required criteria for performance
(What are the required outcomes of
individual performance?)

Collect evidence of outcomes of individual
performance

Match evidence to specified outcomes

Make judgement regarding achievement of
all required performance outcomes

Allocate 'competent' or 'not yet competent'
rating

If purpose of
assessment is
certification

Issue certificate(s) for
achieved competence

Plan development for areas
in which 'not yet competent'
decision has been made

Chapter 4 begins with this model and outlines issues relating to setting requirements and planning assessment. The remaining chapters deal with the collection and matching of evidence to the specified standards, and with review and follow-up procedures and processes. Chapter 7 also highlights some of the other issues which may need attention due to the knock-on effect of the introduction of competence-based assessment. The final chapter deals with quality assurance issues.

Examples of current competence-based assessment systems are included to illustrate key points.

4 Setting Criteria for Required Performance

> SUMMARY <

This chapter helps you to familiarize yourself with the structure and content of competence-based standards. It provides guidance on their use and on setting assessment plans for individuals. You will also find help in considering the key factors which can influence effective assessment.

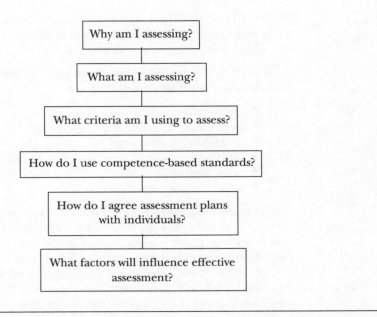

Why am I assessing?

What am I assessing?

What criteria am I using to assess?

How do I use competence-based standards?

How do I agree assessment plans with individuals?

What factors will influence effective assessment?

In Chapter 2, the key features of a competence-based system were outlined. These were

- focus on 'outcomes';
- individualized assessment;
- no percentage rating;
- no comparison with other individuals' results;
- *all* standards (requirements) must be met;
- on-going process – (leads to further development and assessment);
- only 'competent' or 'not yet competent' judgements made.

These key aspects must be borne in mind when considering the specific requirements of performance to be used within a competence-based assessment system.

Your two key questions at this point are *Why am I assessing?* and *What is to be assessed?*

Why Am I Assessing?

In Chapter 2, the key purpose of competence-based assessment was outlined as follows:

To collect sufficient evidence of workplace performance to demonstrate that individuals can perform to the specified standards required within a specified occupational role.

Chapter 3 outlined further, more specific, purposes and uses of competence-based assessment, including:

- certification;
- performance appraisal;
- identifying training needs;
- skills audit;
- prior learning;
- selection and recruitment.

Your overall reason for introducing a competence-based assessment system may be to raise the level of performance within your organization, or to provide a user-friendly and effective system by which performance can be measured and monitored.

You may choose one or any combination of the specific purposes of competence-based assessment listed above to achieve your overall aim, but you must first be clear about your company's key purpose in introducing an assessment system. You need a clear direction before you begin to answer the next question.

What is to be Assessed?

If we are focusing on performance in the workplace, then what you want to assess is that *performance*. But is it the *process of performing* or the *outcome of performance* that you want to assess? Do you want a one-off demonstration of that performance, or do you want to know that people can perform to a specified standard over a period of time? Are you going to assess on an individual or a group basis? Will you need to assess simply *what people do* or also *how well it is done*?

In a competence-based system, as our key features list shows, the focus is on *outcomes* of performance and assessment of *individuals* over a *continuous period*.

A further key point is whether you are assessing competence or excellence. Do you want to set common standards of performance which you can use as a benchmark for competent performers? Do you wish to add a further benchmark of 'excellence'? What are the implications of doing this? If everyone has to meet 'excellent' standards will you be raising the level of performance or risking losing good workers? Will you have a reward system attached to these standards and will excellence gain a higher reward than competence? Is this system to be linked to certification? Is this certification to include national recognition by an external body, or is it to be company certification only?

In a competence-based assessment system, there is no grading of results, only a simple judgement of 'yes you have met the standards' or 'no, you have not met the standards yet'.

In deciding *what* you are going to assess, therefore, you need to begin with the *key aim* of assessment within your company.

Establishing Criteria for Performance

In the UK, national standards of occupational competence for all sectors of industry are being published at all levels. These standards, defined by industry, provide an agreed benchmark of competent performance for occupational roles within each sector.

In the UK, they are also incorporated in the new National Vocational Qualifications. In the USA, similar standards are available as the basis of competency-development programmes. Both forms of standards are illustrated later in this chapter.

These standards will provide you with a sound starting point on which to make your decisions about the standards or criteria for performance which you need to set. They are outcome-based, reflecting expectations

UNIT

ELEMENTS

Manual metal arc welding - 1

- Use electric arc welding safety equipment and protective clothing
- Prepare equipment for manual metal arc welding
- Position work for welding
- Produce welds using manual metal arc welding equipment
- Finish off welding activity

Element 6.1 : Use electric arc welding safety equipment and protective clothing

Performance criteria:

- With the main electricity supply disconnected, the supply and welding connections and cables are checked for correct connection and insulation free from cracks and kinks
- Any shielding gas bottles are correctly marked, stored and hose connections are in good condition
- The welding return lead clamp is securely connected to the work or where applicable to a specially designed workholder
- Fume extraction is working
- The correct filter is in the welders hood
- Screens are available to protect others from arc glare
- Correct safety clothing is worn. This includes safety boots, spats, apron, jerkin, gloves, hat and hood
- Safety glasses are worn when performing any chipping, grinding or dressing
- Safety glasses are worn at all times when welding stainless steel with a slag forming process

Range statement:

Any electric arc welding process for metallic materials, at any level of achievement

Evidence specification:

In addition to meeting the performance criteria of all the elements in this unit, a candidate will have to provide satisfactory answers to the following:

- The reasons for the various storage conditions of different types of coated electrode including basic and cellulosic can be explained
- The reasons for having a sound coating on electrodes can be explained
- The procedure for setting up the type of equipment (ie AC or DC) that has not been demonstrated can be explained
- The causes of slag, spatter, and oxide film can be explained

Figure 4.1 *Example of competence-based standards (UK) – engineering welding (NCVQ 1991)*

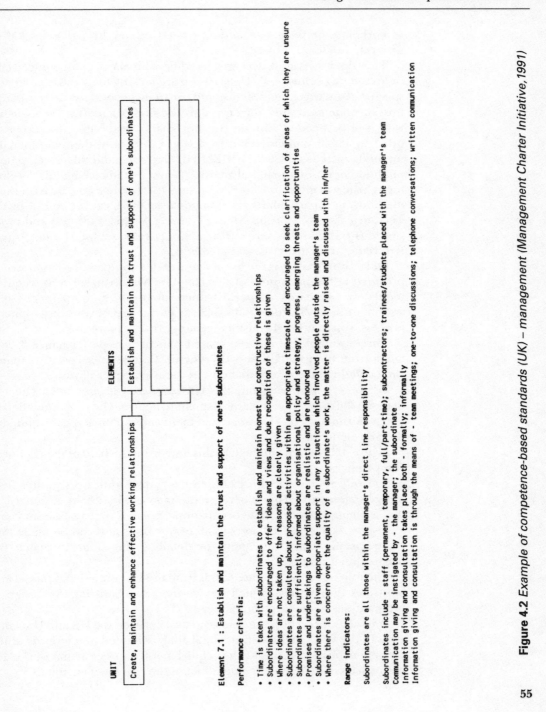

UNIT

Create, maintain and enhance effective working relationships

ELEMENTS

Establish and maintain the trust and support of one's subordinates

Element 7.1 : Establish and maintain the trust and support of one's subordinates

Performance criteria:

• Time is taken with subordinates to establish and maintain honest and constructive relationships
• Subordinates are encouraged to offer ideas and views and due recognition of these is given
• Where ideas are not taken up, the reasons are clearly given
• Subordinates are consulted about proposed activities within an appropriate timescale and encouraged to seek clarification of areas of which they are unsure
• Subordinates are sufficiently informed about organisational policy and strategy, progress, emerging threats and opportunities
• Promises and undertakings to subordinates are realistic and are honoured
• Subordinates are given appropriate support in any situations which involved people outside the manager's team
• Where there is concern over the quality of a subordinate's work, the matter is directly raised and discussed with him/her

Range indicators:

Subordinates are all those within the manager's direct line responsibility

Subordinates include - staff (permanent, temporary, full/part-time); subcontractors; trainees/students placed with the manager's team
Communication may be instigated by - the manager; the subordinate
Information giving and consultation takes place both - formally; informally
Information giving and consultation is through the means of - team meetings; one-to-one discussions; telephone conversations; written communication

Figure 4.2 *Example of competence-based standards (UK) – management (Management Charter Initiative, 1991)*

of workplace performance, and have been agreed through consultation with role holders.

They do, however, reflect an agreed benchmark of competence (UK) or 'excellent performers' (USA). If you are seeking to establish company-specific standards of excellence and/or to incorporate your company's mission statement and objective into the final standards, then further work will be needed. Should you not wish to make use of national or other available standards, but to develop your own, then you may use methods such as DACUM or DELPHI. Current standards development methodology uses functional analysis. General guidance on this develop-ment issue was given in Chapter 3 (page 42). Further guidance on these methods, and particularly on functional analysis, can be found in the Technical Advisory Group Notes (Training Agency 1988–90) and in my previous book in this series, *Designing Competence-based Training* – (see Reference and Further Reading section).

Of key importance is the list of features of a competence-based system provided at the beginning of this chapter. When you set your 'require-ments' or 'standards' of performance for use in a competence-based system, these key features must form a central part of your development process. You may need consultancy support to achieve this.

Three examples of outcome-based standards of performance follow, taken from both the UK and US systems. Competence-based standards can be defined for all occupations, as these examples illustrate.

Figure 4.1 is taken from the UK standards programme. The top diagram illustrates the unit and element structure. The remainder details the performance criteria, range statement and evidence specification for the first element.

Figure 4.2 is also from the UK, this time from the field of management competences.

You will notice that this example has 'range indicators' rather than 'range statements'. This is because the management field is 'generic' – that is, managers work in all occupational areas. Range indicators there-fore serve as a guide for users in all occupations and can be made into more specific range statements by detailing the range to match the occupational context.

The third example (Figure 4.3) is from the US competency model and illustrates the 'clusters' which can be used as a basis for the design of programmes to develop competence.

You will notice a difference in structure between the UK and US stand-ards. In the UK, the use of functional analysis has led to standards which are very explicit in terms of the required outcomes of actual workplace performance while the US system focuses on 'personal attributes'.

Human resource management cluster

Managers with these competencies have positive expectations about others; have realistic views of themselves; build networks or coalitions with others to accomplish tasks, and stimulate cooperation and pride in work groups.

Accurate self-assessment
    The ability to appraise one's strengths and weaknesses realistically.

Self-control
    The ability to subordinate one's personal needs or desires to those of the organization.

Stamina and adaptability
    The ability to sustain long hours of work and be flexible in adapting to change.

Perceptual objectivity
    The ability to be relatively objective about others' views and not limited by subjectivity.

Positive regard
    The ability to express a belief in others' ability to perform and to improve.

Managing the group process
    The ability to stimulate others to work effectively together in a group setting.

Use of socialized power
    The ability to influence others through group effort.

Figure 4.3 *Example of competency-based standards (USA) – human resource management cluster*

There have been criticisms of both systems. Some believe that the UK system focuses too much on the performance of work activities and not enough on the personal effectiveness of individuals. Others believe that the US system focuses too much on personal effectiveness and not enough on the work activities. The UK system does have a set of 'personal competences' – illustrated at Figure 4.6 in the following section. As you will see, this structure is similar to that used in the USA.

Your choice for use of standards must depend upon the objectives of your assessment system. Guidance on the purpose and objectives of assessment systems was given in Chapter 2. You might like to review that chapter before continuing with any plans for introducing a competence-based assessment system.

As a general guide, if you are aiming to assess the actual outcomes of workplace activity, the UK structure illustrated provides a basis on which this can be implemented. If you are seeking to assess personal effectiveness, then the US themes and clusters, or the UK personal competence model would be more appropriate.

Using Standards of Competence

Standards of occupational competence, whether in UK or US format, provide guidance to the assessor on three key aspects of competent performance:

	UK	USA
What has to be achieved	Element	Cluster
How well it must be achieved	Performance criteria	Competency
In what contexts/conditions	Range Statement	Descriptor

Within this system, assessors will assess the elements or clusters of competence, performance criteria and range statements. A number of elements or clusters grouped together form the first level of certification within a vocational award.

Individuals must demonstrate evidence which can be matched to *all* specified standards, across the full specified *range* of activities. This is because a 'competent individual' is someone who can perform:

- to the specified standards;
- consistently;
- over a range of contexts or conditions.

Examples of the structure of standards of competence are given in the following figures.

Fig 4.4 illustrates how the structure of standards fits into a unit and finally a qualification framework. A number of standards – each comprised of an element, performance criteria and range statement – collectively form a unit of competence. A number of units collectively form a qualification.

Figure 4.5 illustrates the framework for the US competency system. This uses 'themes' and 'clusters' to illustrate the areas of competence required. This framework is similar to the UK personal competences model shown in Figure 4.6 and focuses on 'competence' as a personal attribute, rather than an expectation of workplace performance.

Figure 4.6 illustrates the UK personal competence model. As noted above, it is much easier to see similarity between this and the US themes and clusters illustrated in Figure 4.5.

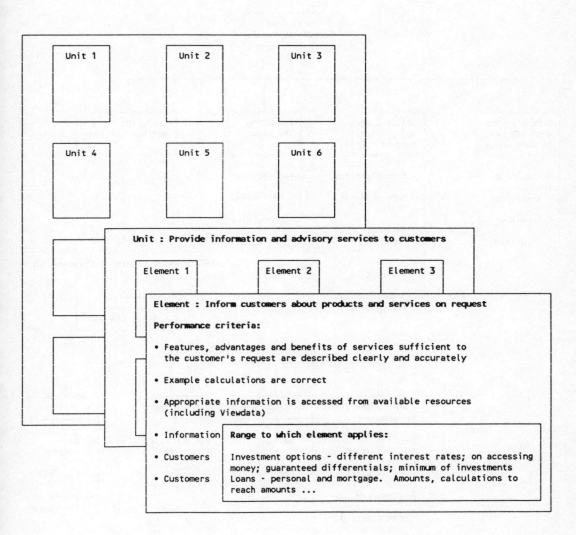

Figure 4.4 *Structure of standards within the retail sector (UK) (Training Agency 1990)*

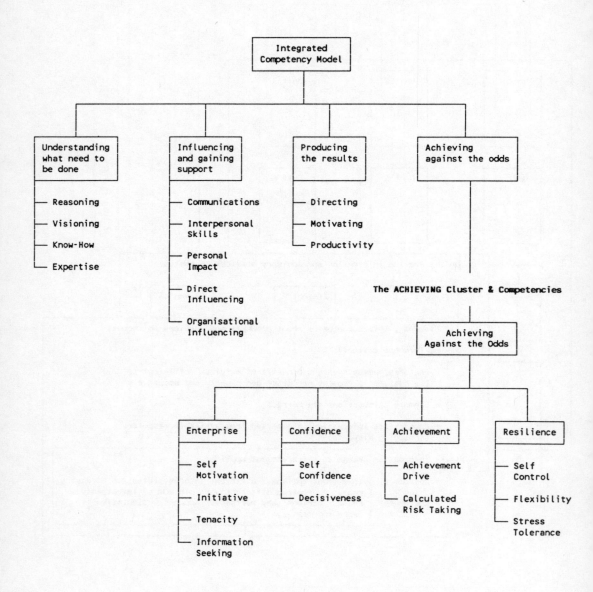

Figure 4.5 *Structure of competency descriptors (USA)*

PERSONAL COMPETENCE MODEL

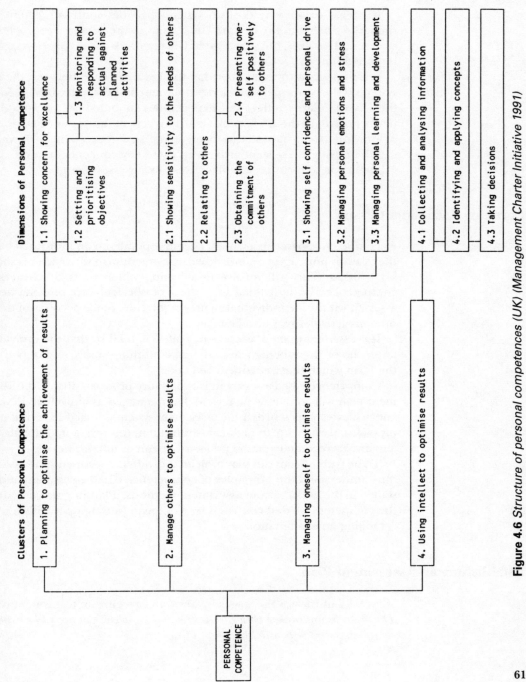

Figure 4.6 *Structure of personal competences (UK) (Management Charter Initiative 1991)*

It is easy to see why the two systems become confused. There are similarities between the US and UK systems in the personal competence structure. However, the structure of UK standards for occupational roles is quite different.

It is important to remember that the key difference between the two systems is the concept on which development of the standards is based. In the UK, standards reflect the expectations or outcomes of workplace performance; in the US system, standards reflect the personal attributes of individuals who have already been recognized as excellent performers.

When using these standards, keep these key concepts in mind. This will help you to focus on the objectives of your assessment.

Agreeing Assessment Plans

As competence-based assessment systems operate on an individual basis, the assessor must agree an individual assessment plan with each person to be assessed. This will involve establishing which units or clusters of competence the individual and the assessor feel can be realistically assessed within the individual's current job role. Some account of development activities may also be taken.

It is essential that an assessment plan is agreed so that the individual knows he or she is being assessed on a continuous basis, and is aware of the form which that assessment will take.

Competence-based assessment is an iterative process – that is, the assessment plan will constantly be reviewed and updated as individuals develop and achieve competence. If the assessment system is linked to certification processes, particularly to national certification, this review and update will also involve recommendation for award of unit or full certificates.

To be truly effective in planning an individual assessment, the assessor must understand the principles of competence-based assessment and be skilled in the use of various assessment methods. 'Planning assessment' in the competence-based context does not mean 'setting up a skills test' or arranging an examination.

Establishing an Assessment Plan

Figure 4.7 illustrates the stages involved in agreeing an assessment plan. *This must be undertaken with each individual for whom you have line management/assessment responsibility.*

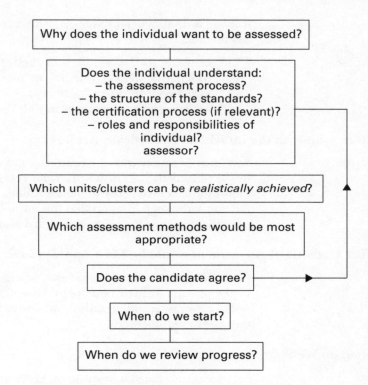

Figure 4.7 *Establishing an assessment plan*

The following text uses the term 'unit' to refer to the first level of assessment which leads to achievement of formal recognition. Readers using a US system should therefore substitute 'cluster' for 'unit'.

Why does the Individual Want to be Assessed?

You must first agree on the reasons for assessment. Is the individual keen to achieve national certification? Are they seeking promotion? Are they seeking training and development?

Does the Individual Understand the System?

Make sure the individual understands the structure of the units and the standards on which they are built. Also check that the individual understands what is involved in the assessment process – that he/she will be assessed on a continuous, not a one-off, basis. The roles and responsibilities of the individual and the assessor must be made clear. (The assessor's role will be outlined in Chapter 5.) The individual's role and responsibilities include:

- bringing to the attention of their designated assessor, evidence which they feel is relevant to on-going assessment (including evidence from past experience);
- agreeing an assessment plan with the line manager.

Which Units can the Individual Realistically Achieve?

You must negotiate with the candidate the number of units which realistically reflects their *current* work role. You may also work with them to identify units which relate to their training or future development needs, but you must keep in mind that the individual must be in a position, or have the opportunity, to provide actual *evidence* of performance.

What Methods of Assessment would be Most Appropriate?

As we have noted already, *observation of natural workplace performance* must be the primary form of assessment. However, you should consider operational constraints and identify those areas which may require supplementary assessment methods.

When do We Start?

Set a clear start date for assessment. Make sure the assessment records are ready for use (including the awarding body log book if appropriate). It is essential that clear and accurate records of assessment are kept, although the system does not have to be elaborate and should be user-friendly. If you are working within an assessment system linked to formal recognition by an awarding body then you may find that pro forma for assessment records are provided by that awarding body. Of course, if you are using your own company system, your documentation will have been devised and developed in-house.

Influences on Assessment

When planning assessment, the assessor must be aware of various influences on the assessment process. The following should be used as a general guidance note in this respect.

Assessment should be *unobtrusive* and should not interfere with normal workplace activity. All assessors can be influenced by a number of factors and it is helpful to be aware of the most common influences so that you can try to avoid them.

A Sense of Direction

Unplanned assessment will result in inaccurate judgements. Always be clear about what evidence you are looking for in any assessment situation. This means being familiar with and understanding the specified standards.

An Illusion of Validity

It is very easy to observe someone or to review written evidence and conclude that 'this is good'. The issue at hand is not whether or not an individual does 'good work'; the issue is whether the evidence you are *currently assessing* provides *valid proof* that the required standards are being met. Evidence can be of high quality but have nothing whatsoever to do with the particular area of competence which you are assessing!

Stereotyping

Sterotyping is never useful in an assessment situation. Your concern as an assessor is to collect and evaluate relevant evidence of actual performance. This has nothing to do with categorizing people.

Halo and Horns Effects

A very common source of inaccurate judgement is due to preconceived ideas about a person's performance. These ideas may be based on the fact that you actually like the person concerned (they have a halo), or that you don't like them (they have horns) – or that they usually do good or excellent work. The reverse works as well: maybe they do or don't like you! None of these considerations should affect your judgement. Your concern is the actual evidence presented.

Hawthorn effect

People act differently when they know they are being assessed. Competence-based assessment is *continuous* and should therefore be carried out under normal working conditions on an everyday basis. We have already noted that assessment should also be unobtrusive.

Contrast Effects

Competence-based assessment is *individualized* assessment. It is concerned with individual performance, not a comparison or contrast with how other people perform. You should be careful to avoid comparing and contrasting the group of candidates for whom you are responsible.

▶ **REVIEW** ◀

This chapter has taken you through the initial steps of competence-based assessment – setting criteria and establishing an action plan. The following chapter moves on to consider the actual collection of evidence.

5 Collecting Evidence of Competence

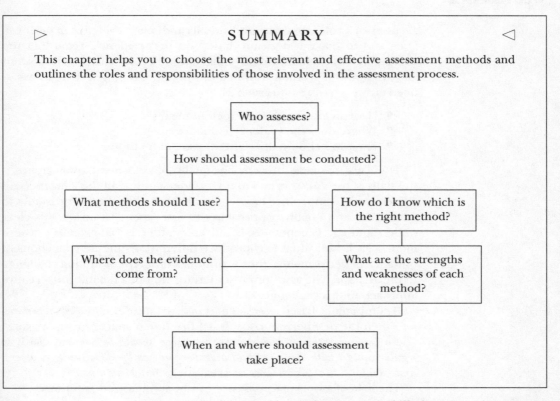

△ SUMMARY ◁

This chapter helps you to choose the most relevant and effective assessment methods and outlines the roles and responsibilities of those involved in the assessment process.

```
                    ┌─────────────────┐
                    │  Who assesses?  │
                    └─────────────────┘
          ┌──────────────────────────────────────┐
          │ How should assessment be conducted?   │
          └──────────────────────────────────────┘
  ┌───────────────────────────┐      ┌──────────────────────┐
  │ What methods should I use? │──────│ How do I know which is │
  └───────────────────────────┘      │   the right method?    │
                                     └──────────────────────┘
  ┌───────────────────────────┐      ┌──────────────────────┐
  │  Where does the evidence   │──────│ What are the strengths │
  │      come from?            │      │ and weaknesses of each │
  └───────────────────────────┘      │        method?         │
                                     └──────────────────────┘
          ┌──────────────────────────────────────┐
          │ When and where should assessment      │
          │           take place?                 │
          └──────────────────────────────────────┘
```

Assessment is about making judgements. A skilled assessor, in any context, is one who is able to review evidence which has been presented and make a confident decision of 'competent' or 'not yet competent' based on that review.

Assessors must be able to establish and agree a clear *assessment plan* with individuals. They must also be aware of *influences on assessment*. These issues were dealt with in Chapter 4.

All of this also requires, however, that assessors are skilled in the choice of *methods* of assessment and that they understand the strengths and weaknesses of each method. They must also be aware of the *sources* of evidence

In this chapter, we look at the who, when, where and how of competence-based assessment. We explore the roles of assessors and methods of assessment together with the strengths and weaknesses of each.

Who Assesses?

An assessor's role is to review individual candidates' evidence of performance and to make a decision, based on that evidence, regarding the competence of each individual in his/her work role. This is an important and responsible position in which to operate. To be effective, assessors need answers to questions such as:

- How do I know what competent means?
- Where does the evidence come from?
- How do I choose the right assessment methods?

There are no magic answers. The quality of assessment however, lies in the skills of the assessors and in their understanding of the concepts and principles of competence-based assessment. A skilled assessor is able to adopt new and creative approaches to assessment based on this clear understanding. Competence-based assessment is *individualized* assessment – each individual may produce different or unique collections of evidence of performance, thus providing a different or unique challenge to the assessor. The assessor must therefore adopt a flexible and creative approach to this challenge.

If competence-based assessment is *individualized* and *focused on performance* then the best person to assess is a first-line manager or supervisor.

An assessor within a competence-based system should be someone who is in regular contact with the individual and therefore has the opportunity to observe and monitor actual performance in a realistic *working environment.*

The role of a workplace assessor can be summarized as follows:

- A workplace assessor is usually a line manager – because a line manager is the best person to observe natural workplace performance.

- The workplace assessor is responsible for collecting *evidence of performance* and ensuring that this evidence is of the correct *type* and *quality* to ensure that a confident judgement of success in required standards is achieved.
- The workplace assessor may use a range of assessment methods but the primary form of assessment must always be *observation of performance*. *Feedback* should be given to individuals on a regular basis and *training needs* will be identified during the course of assessment.
- The workplace assessor is also responsible for *recording assessment*. Details of evidence must be entered on an assessment record.

This creates a new perspective in many organizations. In a competence-based system, the workplace assessor will be a line manager; all line managers must therefore be trained in the skills and application of competence-based assessment. This has considerable long-term benefits: managers become more effective at measuring and managing performance and operate on a more people-oriented basis. A learning culture also develops. However, achievement of these outcomes requires an initial investment in the training of line managers. This issue was illustrated in the Whitbread case study (p. 35) and is also a key point for British Telecom, whose case study follows. (The knock-on effects of introducing competence-based assessment are also outlined in more detail in Chapter 7.)

Case Study: British Telecom

The trainer-training groups in British Telecom decided to go for a competence-based assessment approach as it offered a complete assessment approach and therefore helped to avoid duplication of assessment in a variety of roles. British Telecom used to operate a category system for trainers where the same skills may be used within a particular category, but with a different emphasis.

British Telecom found that 20 activities (competences) previously identified by in-house research would fit into the national system of assessment.

The key difficulty of introducing competence-based assessment, from the viewpoint of British Telecom, is that of training the workplace managers in the principles of the new system.

Managers will need to be very clear about what it is they are looking for; they will need to apply common standards and to give feedback in a developmental way.

British Telecom provides training for managers in training manager support workshops but believes it is also helpful if the workplace managers undertake some of the 20 identified activities themselves on the trainer development programme.

A clear decision has been made that assessment will be undertaken by line managers. Issues of quality and relevance will be uppermost within British Telecom and it is expected that central monitoring of standards will remain an in-house priority.

Accreditation of prior learning will, it is believed, be a part of the assessment system. Plans to operate this in the most cost-effective and efficient way will be considered.

Multiple Assessors

When we talk of a workplace assessor, we usually refer to a 'designated' assessor. Within a competence-based assessment system, each individual should have a designated assessor responsible for recording evidence and 'signing off' satisfactory achievement of competence within a particular area (usually a unit) of competence.

However, as we shall see when we look at sources of evidence (p. 72) a number of assessors can (and often should) be involved in the assessment process. Many people may observe an individual's performance – senior managers, peers, trainers and tutors; all have relevant evidence. An assessor may use these other people as sources of evidence, or they may take a more formal role in supplying evidence on a regular basis. As a rule of thumb, one should remember that the use of multiple assessors can increase the reliability of assessment. However, to keep communication lines clear, only one assessor should have the responsibility for formally recording achievement. (Note also the use of the term 'achievement' rather than 'completion' – this helps to keep your mind focused on *outcomes* rather than training or learning *inputs*.)

How does the Assessor Know what 'Competent' Means?

The assessor in a competence-based system is guided in the assessment process by the specified standards of performance. These were outlined in Chapter 4.

Key Issues for Assessors

Assessment is about *generating* and *collecting* evidence. Different methods of assessment can be used, at different times, to produce evidence of different types.

There are many assessment methods. For example:

- observation of performance;
- skills test;
- simulation exercise;
- project or assignment;
- oral questioning;
- written examination;
- multiple-choice question paper.

Some of these methods provide evidence of *performance*, some provide evidence of *knowledge* and/or *application of knowledge and understanding*.

Assessors may use all or only a few of these. Decisions on which methods to use and on how and when to use them will be influenced by four key components:

- what is to be assessed (the standards);
- the assessment framework (the units);
- the context of assessment (operational constraints);
- skills of the assessor.

The first component – what is to be assessed – was explored in Chapter 4. Competence-based assessment must always start with specified standards of performance. If you are not using nationally agreed standards, then your own must be in a format which clearly indicates the *outcomes* which individuals must achieve.

The second component – the assessment framework – again depends upon the system you are using. In the UK certification system of National Vocational Qualifications, your framework will consist of *units of competence*. If you are using a different model, your framework may be *clusters of behaviour*. Whatever your system, it should be in usable chunks – each chunk representing an area of activity which has real meaning in the workplace. This is essential if you are linking your assessment to certification and reward systems.

The third component – the context of assessment – is crucial to the successful operation of your assessment scheme. In an ideal situation, each individual to be assessed will have a line manager as a designated assessor. Each designated assessor will be monitored by a verifier (see Chapter 8), and each verifier will in turn be monitored by an external verifier. However, ideal situations do not often exist!

Your particular operational constraints must be taken into account and issues such as lines of communication and accountability must be paramount in these considerations. But these are not the only issues: operational constraints affect the choice of assessment methods, and assessors will need to tailor the choice of assessment method to the operational context.

The skills of the assessor – the fourth component – are therefore of utmost importance, which is why assessors will need training and development (see Chapter 8). Assessors need skills in the selection and use of assessment methods, and they need an understanding of the strengths and weaknesses of each method. They also need to make the best use of various sources of evidence in addition to being fully aware of the many influences on assessment. The remainder of this chapter deals with these issues.

Sources of Evidence

In order to select the most appropriate and effective assessment methods, an assessor must have a clear understanding of the various sources of evidence. This section reviews the following key sources of evidence of performance:

- multiple assessors;
- performance at work;
- specially set tasks/projects/ assignments;
- questioning;
- historical evidence.

Multiple assessors

Earlier in this chapter, we briefly reviewed the idea of multiple assessors – a variety of people who have contact with the individual being assessed and who therefore can provide evidence of that individual's performance. One *source* of evidence, therefore, is other people who have this contact.

If we are to make best use of this source, however, we need to have clear lines of communication. People need to know that they have a role in providing evidence.

In your own context, consider who these people might be. For example:

- senior managers;
- tutors and trainers;
- peers and co-workers;

- customers;
- contacts in other divisions/departments.

Basically, anyone with whom an individual has contact within their normal working activity can be a source of evidence. But take care – your approach to each source will need to be planned. You will also need to make sure that the evidence you receive reflects the performance of the particular individual, and is not clouded by that person's involvement in team activities. All sources must be carefully considered in terms of the quality of evidence provided. (The issue of quality is dealt with in the next chapter.)

Performance at work

The best evidence comes from actual workplace performance. Remember, competence-based standards reflect *outcomes* of performance; where better to collect evidence of achievement of these outcomes than in the realistic, everyday working environment?

Observation of actual workplace performance should always be an assessor's primary *form of evidence collection.*

Performance on Specially Set Tasks

Where observation of normal workplace activity is not possible, special tasks or assignments can be set to *generate* the required evidence. Because it is produced in a 'false' or 'simulated' setting, evidence provided by this route will not be of the same high quality as that generated by normal workplace activity. However, evidence produced by simulated methods will contribute to continuous assessment and help the assessor make decisions about the individual's competence across the specified range of activities.

There are times when a simulation or skills test or project will be an essential means of generating evidence. For example, an assessor cannot set fire to a building, or shut down equipment and machinery to assess whether an individual knows how to deal with such an emergency. Similarly, where licensing is required, such as with fork lift truck drivers, health and safety requirements would prohibit assessment in real working situations until the licence had been obtained.

Other issues also come into play. Competence-based assessment requires that individuals are assessed across the full range of activities specified within the standards. Individuals do not always have the opportunity to demonstrate their competence on all types of equipment or machinery. For example, a welder may need to demonstrate competence in the use of MIG, TIG and arc welding, but may not have an opportunity to do so for some time if the particular work in hand requires only two out of the three methods. In this type of circumstance, use of specially set tasks, projects, assignments and tests can generate the evidence required.

Questioning

It is often the case that observation of normal activity and specially set tasks do not provide sufficient evidence. For example, if an individual needs to be assessed across a wide range of contexts or conditions, or in the use of a wide range of equipment or machinery, the assessor may have to spend years waiting for, or trying to create, the right opportunity!

In assessing competence, the assessor is attempting to collect evidence that demonstrates an individual's performance to required standards. This includes *application* of knowledge and understanding – it is not 'knowing' itself that is important in competent performance, but what individuals *do* with that knowledge.

If you want to know that an individual is able to drive a car on a clear day, with little traffic about, you might observe their performance by sitting in the car with them. However, if you also want to know that they can drive the same car, or different cars, in rain, snow, sleet, hail, high winds, thunderstorms, in light and heavy traffic, and on motorways, A and B roads and dirt tracks, you might take years to assess them this way!

Your basic aim as an assessor in this context, and in all other competence-based assessments, is to collect sufficient evidence to make a confident judgement that the individual can perform to the required standards across the full range of specified activities.

One very simple way of finding out what you need to know is to ask. In the assessment context, your questions need to be carefully framed to elicit the *evidence* you are seeking. You might ask 'What if…' to elicit evidence of performance across the range of activity. You might set a series of open, written questions to assess that an individual is able to apply relevant knowledge and understanding to activities which require decision-making, or problem-solving. For example, assessing a doctor's performance across the full range of diagnoses, medicines and medical tests applied to patients could take forever unless a written form of evidence collection was used!

Historical evidence

The term 'historical evidence' has been used to refer to evidence of past achievements and often occurs in literature and guidance on the accreditation of prior learning (APL).

Evidence from past achievements can be valuable in competence-based assessment and often forms part of the on-going assessment process.

Again, the *quality* of evidence is of paramount importance and the 'rules of evidence' must apply (see Chapter 6).

In a sense, we might say that all evidence is historical, since once it has been produced it is immediately in the past! However, this source of evidence can, when used effectively, help to fill the gaps when an assessor is attempting to collect evidence across the full range of an activity.

Choosing the Right Assessment Methods

Assessment methods include:

- observation of performance;
- skills tests;
- simulation exercises;
- project or assignment;
- oral questioning;
- written examination;
- multiple-choice question paper.

We noted earlier that some of these methods provide evidence of *performance* and some provide evidence of *knowledge and understanding*. You will also recall that it is *application* of knowledge and understanding that is of key interest in a competence-based assessment system.

When considering the use of various assessment methods, an assessor must keep these questions in mind:

- What evidence do I need?
- How much evidence do I need?
- Which methods will provide quality evidence?

The following pages provide guidance on the use of each of the assessment methods listed above, with these key questions in mind. This guidance refers to the selection of assessment methods; guidance on quality of evidence follows in Chapter 6.

Observation of Performance

Strengths
- Provides high quality evidence of competence.
- Is undertaken (or should be) as usual part of line manager's responsibility.

- Individuals become accustomed to on-going assessment.
- Provides continuous assessment basis.
- Evidence is produced regardless of whether it is used for assessment.

Weaknesses
- Opportunities to demonstrate competence across full range of activities may be limited.
- Interference of 'local' standards/procedures may affect time allocated to workplace assessment.
- Assessor/assessee relationship.

Key Issues
- Need for trained assessors.
- Use of multiple assessors.
- Need for clear lines of communication and quality-assurance measures.

Specially Set Tasks: Skills Tests, Simulations, Projects, Assignments

Strengths
- A useful tool for generating evidence where opportunities for assessment across the full range are limited or prohibited by health and safety regulations.
- Can be off-site and therefore avoid noisy or disruptive environments.
- Test conditions can be standardized for skills tests.
- Time for testing can be effectively allocated.

Weaknesses
- Removed from realistic working conditions.
- Individuals react differently in a test situation.
- Structure of assignments and projects often very loose.
- Difficulties in predicting exactly what type of evidence will be generated.

Key Issues
- Need for planning and structure.

Oral Questioning

Strengths
- Valuable tool for collecting evidence across full range of activities (ie, providing supplementary evidence).

- Valuable tool for collecting evidence of underpinning knowledge and understanding and its application in the workplace.
- Can be rigorous, and standardized with planning and structure.

Weaknesses
- Assessors can often answer their own questions!
- Evidence collected by this method alone would not be sufficient to assign competence.
- Least likely to reflect or represent real working conditions.

Key Issues
- Need for trained assessors with effective questioning techniques.
- Requires largest inferential jump to assigning competence.

Written Examination

Strengths
- Valuable tool for assessment in areas where knowledge forms a key component of competent performance (eg, information providers).
- Can be well structured to elicit key areas of knowledge and understanding.

Weaknesses
- Also assesses ability to write and construct written material.
- Needs skilled assessors to judge responses.
- Time away from workplace required to complete the examination.
- Time for assessors to review and mark responses.

Key Issues
- Danger of assumption that 'knowing' means 'able to do'.
- Often unstructured or unplanned.
- Supplies supplementary evidence of actual performance.

Multiple-choice Question Papers

Multiple-choice question papers provide a useful tool for assessing knowledge of a particular topic. They need careful construction and are usually put together by subject experts who are also skilled in the use of this form of assessment. The basic model of a multiple-choice question paper is, as its name implies, a question followed by several possible answers for the candidates to choose between.

Strengths
- Well-designed questions can be standardized.
- Elicits key knowledge/understanding in short timescale.

Weaknesses
- Always a 25 per cent possibility of correct answer being chosen at random (where four possible answers are given).
- Needs skilled designer to prepare item bank and question paper.
- Time away from work to complete test needed.

Key Issues
- Time and skills needed for design, delivery and marking.
- Supplementary evidence only – not direct evidence of actual performance.

When and Where should Assessment Take Place?

In planning competence-based assessment, one of the key aims should be to make it flexible so that candidates can be assessed in a variety of ways. An assessor should also take into account any operational constraints.

Wherever possible, assessment should take place *in the workplace* with *observation of normal workplace activity*. This may not always be possible, either because the opportunity to assess across the full range of activity is limited, or because the noise within the working environment makes questioning or discussion difficult.

Where assessors are attempting to assess field staff, further difficulties arise. How can a manager assess his staff when they are out at customers' premises all day?

Competence-based assessment may, therefore, take place in the workplace or off the job. It should be continuous, making the best use of naturally occuring evidence (from normal work activity). Assessors will need to be able to set up and manage other forms of assessment, however, in order to ensure that high-quality and sufficient evidence is generated, collected and recorded before competence can be assigned to an individual.

Assessors must first understand the basis on which a competence-based assessment system operates. They must be clear about the principles of assessment and the requirements for high-quality evidence of performance. They must be aware of and develop skill in the use of various assessment methods and be able to use any combination of methods to meet the operational constraints in which they operate. Only when assessors have been trained in these skills can the assessment system operate effectively.

Effective operation begins with the establishment of assessment plans. This planning process was outlined in Chapter 4. The selection and use of assessment methods, and planning of the location and timing, all contribute to the overall quality of the assessment system.

► REVIEW ◄

In this chapter, the process of collecting evidence has been explored. Well-planned collection of evidence is critical to ensure that the right quantity and quality of evidence is available for matching to the specified standards.

Chapter 6 explores the next steps – matching of evidence to standards and making judgements about individual achievement of competence.

---

6 Matching Evidence to Standards

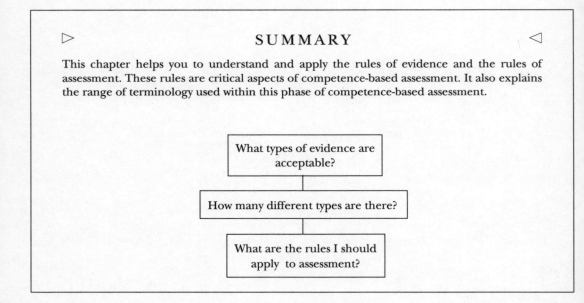

▷ SUMMARY ◁

This chapter helps you to understand and apply the rules of evidence and the rules of assessment. These rules are critical aspects of competence-based assessment. It also explains the range of terminology used within this phase of competence-based assessment.

```
┌─────────────────────────────┐
│  What types of evidence are │
│         acceptable?         │
└─────────────────────────────┘
┌─────────────────────────────┐
│ How many different types are there? │
└─────────────────────────────┘
┌─────────────────────────────┐
│  What are the rules I should │
│     apply  to assessment?   │
└─────────────────────────────┘
```

Introduction

The quality of a competence-based assessment system depends, as we have noted earlier, on the skills of the assessor. A key assessor skill concerns making judgements about the quality of evidence collected. Chapter 5 explored various assessment methods, together with the strengths and weaknesses of each. In this chapter, we look at the quality of evidence which is generated from these various assessment methods.

As a general rule, evidence generated from normal workplace activity will be of the highest quality. We can then move down a scale of quality as illustrated in Figure 6.1 (based on Mitchell (1989)).

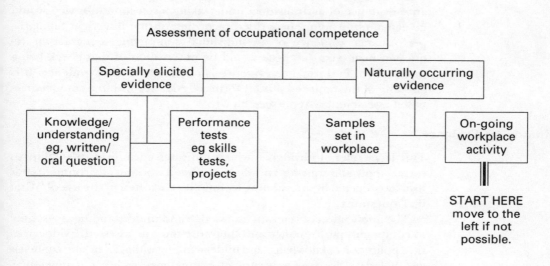

Figure 6.1 *Quality of Evidence of Occupational Competence*

Types of Evidence

Another area of general confusion for those new to competence-based systems occurs when discussions about *types* of evidence takes place. Once again, a variety of terms tends to be used interchangeably, often including:

- performance evidence;
- knowledge evidence;
- direct evidence;
- primary evidence;
- indirect evidence;
- supporting evidence;
- supplementary evidence;
- historical evidence.

In this initial section, these terms will be defined so that further exploration of rules of evidence can be undertaken without the added clutter of confusing terminology.

Performance Evidence

This term has been used in earlier chapters and refers specifically to evidence of an individual *actually doing something*. For example, performance evidence of an individual undertaking a selection interview would be actual observation, or a video recording of that interview. Similarly, performance evidence of an individual completing a regular or requested maintenance check would be observation of that check being undertaken. Performance evidence is one form of *direct* evidence. It is also one of the required *primary* forms of evidence within a competence-based assessment system (see below).

Knowledge Evidence

This term refers to evidence which indicates an individual's ability to recall, apply and transfer knowledge within a working environment. It is usually collected by questioning techniques and often by the use of 'What if…' questions.

The application of relevant knowledge and understanding is essential to competent performance and therefore must be assessed. Evidence of the application of knowledge and understanding within a working context is also a *primary* form of evidence of competence within a competence-based assessment system.

Primary Evidence

The two definitions above referred to this term. Within a competence-based assessment system, the *primary* types of evidence are those which provide information about *actual* performance or the *application* of knowledge and understanding within *realistic* (normal) workplace activity.

Direct Evidence

This is evidence which gives clear information about the candidate's performance. It will take the following forms:

- actual products of performance;
- results of observation of performance;
- results of questioning by the assessor.

These three forms of evidence also represent *primary* evidence (see above).

Direct evidence about some aspects of performance can also be obtained from skills tests, projects and assignments. However, such evidence is usually referred to as *supporting* or *supplementary* evidence (see below).

This is the simplest form of evidence for an assessor to use in matching to standards, but is often the most difficult to collect because of the time required to observe or question the individual or to examine finished products.

Indirect Evidence

Indirect evidence provides the assessor with information *about* the individual and may take the form of:

- references or letters of validation;*
- photographs of completed work;
- audio tapes;
- trophies or awards;
- letters from customers/colleagues;
- production records;
- training records.

Many other forms of evidence may come into this category. It is important to remember that in a competence-based system, an assessor is dealing with *individualized* assessment. This means that the types of evidence presented, particularly where historical evidence is included (see below), will be unpredictable. Assessors must become used to dealing with unfamiliar and new forms of evidence. In this context, confidence in use of the rules of evidence, discussed later in this chapter, is critical to success.

Supporting or Supplementary Evidence

As the terms imply, supporting or supplementary evidence is that which adds to the main (or direct) forms. There is, therefore, some comparison between indirect and supporting and supplementary evidence. These terms are often used interchangeably.

Evidence from skills tests, projects and assignments is often termed supporting or supplementary; this leads to considerable confusion since this type of evidence can also be referred to as 'direct' (see above).

Use of these terms, as in many contexts, depends upon the perspective being adopted. If the discussion concerns the direct/indirect dimensions, then evidence from skills tests, projects and assignments will be direct because the evidence collected in this way *directly* reflects *part of* the required performance. However, if the discussion concerns primary

*A letter of validation is a form of reference, but one which provides specific information relating to the standards of performance. This form of reference is often provided by individuals as part of an accreditation of prior learning process (see 'historical evidence').

versus supporting/supplementary evidence (see above), then skills tests, projects and assignments will be viewed as supporting/supplementary evidence. This is because these test situations are simulated and do not fully reflect realistic workplace activity as it would be undertaken on a normal day-to-day basis.

Historical Evidence

Historical evidence is that which provides the assessor with information about an individual's past achievements. It may take any form and include those listed under the primary, supporting, direct and indirect headings above. Historical evidence therefore can be the most difficult to assess, but it can also provide one of the most valuable sources of evidence. Assessors will need skill and confidence if the credibility and quality of the assessment system is to be maintained.

Methods and Quality

Two sets of rules are applied within a competence-based system. The first refers to the *methods* of assessment and the second to the *quality* of evidence collected.

You might consider these two sets of rules as similar to rules applying to the legal profession.

In a court case, it is possible that *sufficient* evidence has been collected in order for a jury to make a confident judgement about guilt or innocence. However, technicalities relating to *how* the evidence was collected can make the sufficiency issue irrelevant.

The same rules apply in your workplace assessment. You may have sufficient evidence, but if the methods of collecting that evidence were invalid, the quality of evidence is affected.

So how can you ensure quality and sufficiency and thus make confident judgements in your assessment role?

Six key concepts must be kept in mind. These concepts relate both to quality of assessment method used and quality of evidence assessed. They are illustrated in Figure 6.2 and outlined in more detail in the following text.

```
┌─────────────────────────────────────┐
│        Rules of assessment          │
│                                     │
│           Transparency              │
│             Validity                │
│            Reliability              │
└─────────────────────────────────────┘
```

```
┌─────────────────────────────────────┐
│         Rules of evidence           │
│                                     │
│             Validity                │
│           Authenticity              │
│             Currency                │
│            Sufficiency              │
└─────────────────────────────────────┘
```

Figure 6.2 *Key concepts of methods and quality*

Rules for Assessment Methods

Transparency

If something is transparent, it is open and clear to anyone who takes time to look at, or through it. A competence-based assessment system should be clear to all involved. If standards are accessible, easily understood and have real meaning to the users, and if the assessment plans and methods are well thought out then roles and responsibilities are more easily conducted.

Validity

A well planned assessment is one in which the assessor and the individual being assessed are clear on *what* is to be assessed and *what* evidence will be generated. In addition, the types and forms of evidence will provide realistic proof of the specified standards. A common example of invalid assessment (and invalid evidence) would be a written test of practical skill. A *valid* assessment would be observation of reactions to a fire alarm (particularly when the time for testing of the alarm was not known in advance by the individuals).

As an assessor, think firstly of your objectives in assessment. Ask yourself what you need to find out (what evidence you need) about this person's performance. Then ask whether this assessment method will provide that evidence.

Reliability

An assessment system is only of real value if assessors in different locations would make the same judgement about the same candidate based on the same evidence. A well-designed assessment system builds in tests of reliability through quality control and monitoring of assessment. Your in-company assessment scheme will only be reliable if two different assessors provided with the same collection of evidence reach the same conclusion about the competence of the individual to whom the evidence refers. This type of testing activity should form part of assessor training (see Chapter 8).

Rules of Evidence

Validity

The same issue – assessing what is supposed to be assessed – arises when considering evidence. The key question for assessors to ask about each piece of evidence is 'What does this evidence tell me?' It may tell you something about the specified standards or it may tell you about some other related activity.

For example, if you were assessing maintenance engineers, you might receive documentation referring to completed work. What does this documentation tell you? Does it tell you that the work was completed to the correct safety standards? Does it tell you that the work completed was as requested by the customer? Does it tell you that the work was completed using the correct parts and that they were all fitted correctly? Does it tell you if the customer was satisfied?

In fact, the documentation may only tell you that the engineer is able (or not, as the case may be) to complete paperwork correctly, neatly and in accordance with company procedures!

Remember, the issue of validity *is critical. Ask 'What does this piece of evidence actually tell me about this individual's performance?'*

Authenticity

How do you know that the evidence presented to you was actually produced by the named individual? Was it produced by the individual alone, or as part of a team?

These questions are particularly relevant when assessors are dealing with 'historical' evidence, but still have to be kept in mind when current evidence is being considered.

If an assessor is to attribute competence to an individual based on the evidence presented, then the issue of authenticity must be addressed.

Currency

Once again, this is of particular relevance to evidence from prior achievement (historical evidence) but should not be ignored in on-going workplace assessment. The key here is to focus on the standards as your starting point.

It is very easy for assessors to fall into the trap of making assumptions about evidence. This can be due to the many influences on assessment (see page 64), or due to lack of planning of assessment (page 62) or due to lack of application of rules of assessment (page 85). Most often, however, falling into the 'assumption trap' is caused by assessors failing to refer (and to re-refer) to the specified standards as their starting point.

Evidence is only current if the information it provides the assessor matches that specified within the standards.

Sufficiency

Once assessors have managed the collection of evidence and the application of rules of validity, authenticity and currency, one question remains: Do you have *enough* evidence of the right *quality* to make a *confident* judgement about competence?

This question of sufficiency has caused considerable difficulties for new assessors who frequently ask how to decide what is enough.

Here we come back to the key principles of competence-based assessment and to the format which standards of occupational competence take. A basic rule for competence-based assessment is that *all of the standards must be assessed.* This means that evidence must be collected to demonstrate that an individual has performed the element and its associated performance criteria across the full specified range of activity before that *element* can be 'signed off'. In addition, this signing-off activity for each element must be completed before the unit of competence can similarly be signed off and a certificate issued for that unit.

The issue of providing evidence for each performance criterion and across the full range sounds like a horrendous task for assessors. If this task is approached on the basis that one piece of evidence is required for each criterion and for each aspect of the range then this would be true.

However, contrary to general belief, this is not the case. The issue of matching evidence and making judgements about competence is explained in the next section on matching evidence and judging competence.

I end this section with a checklist which I have found very useful for new assessors. It also leads us nicely into the next section.

Applying Rules of Evidence: Checklist for Assessment

- All of the standards must be assessed.
- Evidence should relate clearly and directly to specified standards.
- There should be sufficient evidence to cover the full range of contexts or contingencies specified within the standards.
- There should be no comparison or contrast between candidates – evidence relates directly to individual assessment.
- Evidence should be traceable to its source (effective record keeping is important).
- Evidence should be generated in realistic conditions using valid assessment methods.
- The assessment process should put no additional pressure on candidates or assessor.

Matching Evidence and Judging Competence

The checklist in the previous section forms a useful guide for assessors in the matching and judging stages of competence-based assessment. The following text provides more detail to help assessors use the checklist and thus to develop and maintain confidence in their assessment role.

All of the Standards must be Assessed

Only two judgements are possible in competence-based assessment – 'competent' or 'not yet competent'. Because the performance criteria relate to *critical* aspects of performance, this means that all criteria must be met. Because true competence entails transferability of skills and knowledge, evidence of performance across the specified range must also be collected.

The Evidence should Relate Clearly to the Standards

There are a number of issues relating to rules of evidence. These include validity, currency, authenticity and sufficiency and are discussed earlier in this chapter.

Sufficient Evidence must be Generated in Realistic Conditions

Competence-based assessment assesses *workplace* activity. Assessment should therefore take place in a realistic working environment and relate to normal working practice.

The Assessment Process should be Individualized, but should not Put Additional Pressures on the Candidate

As an assessor, you need to assess each individual in their normal working practice. Assessment should be unobtrusive and should relate only to the specified standards.

The Assessment Process should not Put Additional Pressures on the Assessor

Assessors in competence-based systems are usually line managers. Competence-based standards are designed to make explicit what people do in their normal working roles. They should therefore provide assistance to managers in their supervisory role and not increase their workload to an unmanageable degree.

How Much Evidence?

We come back to the question of sufficiency of evidence and to a concept which assessors invariably find difficult at first. As noted in the first part of this chapter, one misconception which causes problems on the 'sufficiency' front is that one piece of evidence must be found for each performance criterion (Figure 6.3).

In fact, one piece of evidence can provide valid information about more than one performance criterion. It may even provide valid information about performance criteria in different elements, or different units. Figure 6.4 illustrates this.

Assessors have expressed initial concerns that competence-based assessment will generate mountains of paperwork, that each individual will need to collect piles of evidence which has to be stored somewhere and judged on a one-to-one basis with each performance criterion. As Figure 6.4 illustrates, this is not the case. Assessors will only develop the confidence to make such judgements, however, through practice. It becomes clear, therefore, that building such practice into assessor training can help develop this confidence.

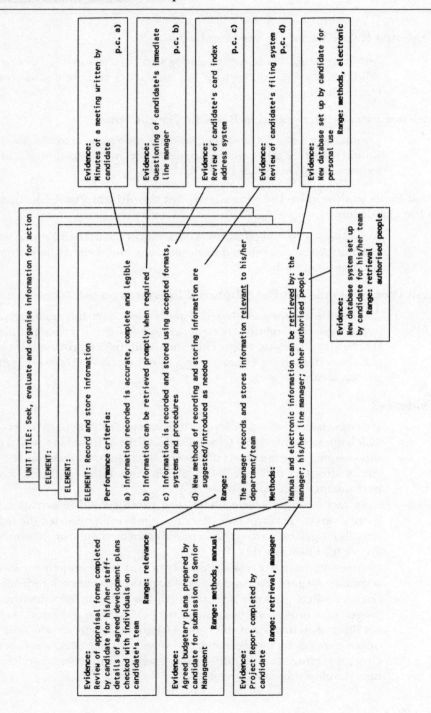

Figure 6.3 *Misconceptions about matching evidence*

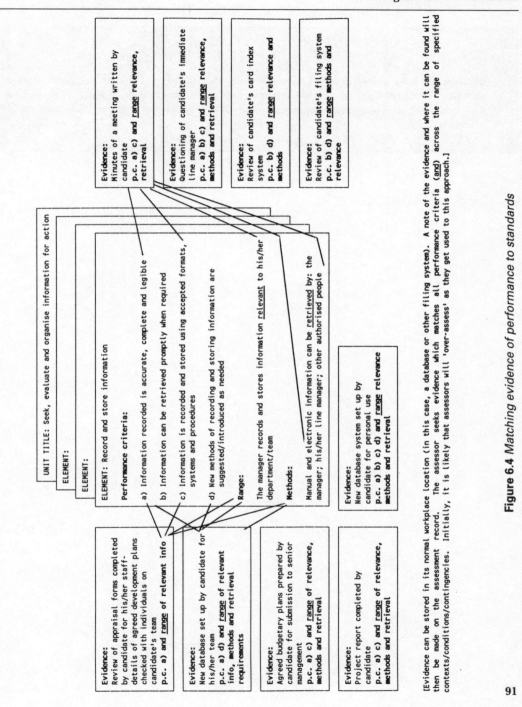

Figure 6.4 Matching evidence of performance to standards

[Evidence can be stored in its normal workplace location (in this case, a database or other filing system). A note of the evidence and where it can be found will then be made on the assessment record. The assessor seeks evidence which matches all performance criteria (and) across the range of specified contexts/conditions/contingencies. Initially, it is likely that assessors will 'over-assess' as they get used to this approach.]

► REVIEW ◄

This chapter has outlined the key issues relating to the matching of evidence of performance standards and explained the many different terms used. All assessment activities should be accompanied by feedback and follow-up action; the next chapter looks at these peripheral activities.

7 Review and Follow-up

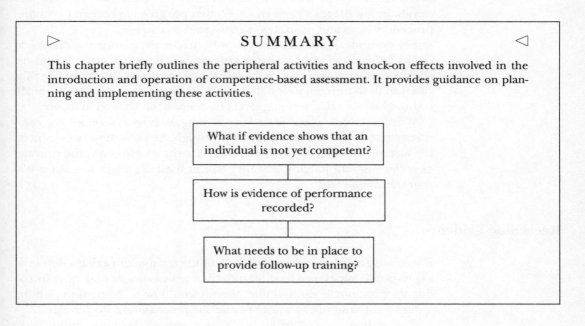

▷ **SUMMARY** ◁

This chapter briefly outlines the peripheral activities and knock-on effects involved in the introduction and operation of competence-based assessment. It provides guidance on planning and implementing these activities.

What if evidence shows that an individual is not yet competent?

How is evidence of performance recorded?

What needs to be in place to provide follow-up training?

Identifying Training Needs

In conducting on-going assessment of performance, an assessor will automatically identify training and development needs. When collecting evidence of performance, 'gaps' in this evidence will emerge. These may be due to lack of opportunity to demonstrate competence. They may also be due, however, to lack of experience, skills or knowledge.

The competence-based assessment system therefore provides a working model for the identification of training needs – as long as the assessor is skilled in recognizing which gaps are due to training needs and which to lack of opportunity!

Such is the 'knock-on effect' of introducing competence-based assessment within an organization. Once supervisors and line managers start to use the assessment system, their skills (or the need to develop them) also receive highlighted attention. Line managers need to develop skills in providing feedback and in recognition of training needs, to name but two.

In addition, the organization's procedures get some attention. It is only when assessors attempt to find quality evidence, and when they begin to ask key questions such as 'What does this evidence actually tell me about Joe Bloggs's performance?' that possible improvements in the procedural and administrative systems start to emerge.

For example, in the last chapter, we considered documentation which might be completed by an engineer and asked what it actually told us about the work completed by the individual engineer. Questions like this can lead us to the conclusion that our recording system is perhaps not all it should be – or that our engineers have not been trained in its use!

When we think about *identifying training needs* therefore, we are considering both assessor and assessee. Through the collection of evidence, the assessor will identify the needs of the assessee. However, the process of collecting and judging evidence will in itself highlight the assessor's own training needs!

Recording Evidence

If your organization is going to go to all the trouble of perhaps developing its own competence-based standards and assessment system, or introducing a nationally devised one, then it would be a shame if the whole system was found not to work because the records were inadequate.

The system for recording evidence needs to be both simple and efficient. Assessors need space to record *what* evidence they have collected, *where* they collected it, *when* they collected it and the *method of assessment* used. These facts need to be recorded for each element of competence. There also needs to be space for the assessor to record that the element has been achieved (when sufficient, high-quality evidence has been collected and matched to the specified standards).

These records may be used, within a national, organizational or professional vocational qualification system, as the basis for recommendation

Candidate name: _____ Unit number: _____ Element number: _____

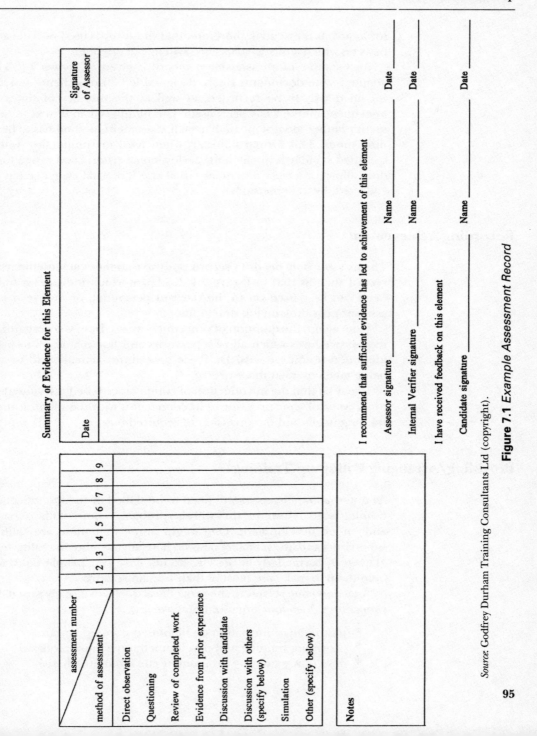

assessment number	1	2	3	4	5	6	7	8	9
method of assessment									
Direct observation									
Questioning									
Review of completed work									
Evidence from prior experience									
Discussion with candidate									
Discussion with others (specify below)									
Simulation									
Other (specify below)									

Date	Summary of Evidence for this Element	Signature of Assessor

I recommend that sufficient evidence has led to achievement of this element

Assessor signature _____ Name _____ Date _____

Internal Verifier signature _____ Name _____ Date _____

I have received feedback on this element

Candidate signature _____ Name _____ Date _____

Notes

Source: Godfrey Durham Training Consultants Ltd (copyright).

Figure 7.1 *Example Assessment Record*

for award. It is essential, therefore, that the records used provide a solid basis on which a quality-assurance system can operate.

An example of an assessment record is given in Figure 7.1. This is adapted from documents I have designed for various clients and allows for all details to be recorded, as well as the number of times each assessment method has been used. The numbers 1 to 9 next to 'assessment number' do not mean that each assessment method has to be used nine times! This format however, when used in conjunction with the specified standards in element, performance criteria and range format, does allow for a clear and quick visual check of what evidence has been collected, by what methods.

Recording Achievement

The assessor only needs to record positive evidence (achievement) on a record such as that in Figure 7.1. Evidence which indicates a training need can be passed on to the relevant personnel, or may lead to the assessor providing on-job development.

Here again, the question of procedures arises. Does your organization have procedures which allow supervisors and line managers to pass on identified training needs? Do these procedures actually lead to action being taken to meet those needs?

It may be that the introduction of competence-based assessment leads to a review of your procedures in connection with the identification of training needs and the provision of required training.

Providing/Arranging Follow-up Training

As noted above, assessors will need to be skilled in the identification of training needs. However, they will also probably require skills in coaching and on-job development. One might argue that these are skills that supervisors and line managers should have anyway – but in reality, few do. Managers, particularly in the UK, do not have key 'people skills' which help them to make the most of their human resource.

A second issue relates to the procedural question already raised. What procedures does your organization have for:

- passing up information on identified training need?
- providing training and development on a modular basis?
- developing training programmes on a modular basis?

- designing and developing programmes based on explicit standards of performance?

Again, the knock-on effect of introducing competence-based assessment begins to become clear.

If the assessment system is to be used to the full, then supporting systems of training and development for all staff, including those who take on an assessor role, must be put in place. A competence-based assessment system provides a valuable foundation on which to measure, manage and maintain high-quality performance within an organization. However, this can only happen if the implications of introducing the system are carefully considered and plans for peripheral activities are put into action at an early stage.

The final issue to be addressed is that of quality assurance. Chapter 8 explains the key issues and provides general guidance on this matter.

▶ **REVIEW** ◀

This chapter has outlined the peripheral issues of recording assessment and quality assurance. Although 'peripheral', these issues should not be dismissed! Any assessment system is only as good as its supporting infrastructure. You should, therefore, give careful thought to the design of your supporting framework and its operation.

8 Quality-assurance Issues

▷ **SUMMARY** ◁

This final chapter outlines the key issues relating to quality assurance. It provides a basic (national) quality-assurance model with guidance on how this might be adapted to operate at corporate or departmental level.

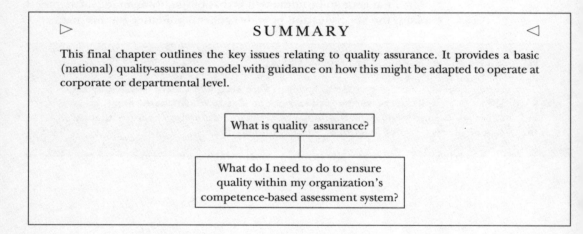

What is quality assurance?

What do I need to do to ensure quality within my organization's competence-based assessment system?

Introduction

There is little point in developing and introducing a competence-based assessment system unless an effective quality assurance model is put in place to ensure that standards, and the credibility of the system are maintained.

There are several aspects to quality assurance within competence-based assessment systems. These vary depending upon whether your organization introduces a nationally approved system, such as that relating to National Vocational Qualifications (NVQs) in the UK, or whether you operate your own in-house system.

However, whether your system operates in-house, and with or without certification, key issues to be addressed in the design and/or establishment of a quality assurance system will be:

- selection of assessors;
- training of assessors;
- monitoring of assessors.

If your system is also linked to certification, either in-house or national, other issues will need to be addressed, such as approval of assessment sites, and procedures for certification.

All these issues are dealt with in the following sections.

Selection of Assessors

Assessors are key personnel within a competence-based assessment system. You will wish to consider the main characteristics/technical requirements for assessors within your organization. If you operate within a national certification system, you may well find that the selection criteria are already established; nevertheless, these criteria will include the following:

- experience in the occupational role;
- experience in supervision/line management;
- willingness to undertake assessment.

The last may seem strange, but it is essential. If line managers are not willing to undertake assessment, then they will not undertake the assessment thoroughly, and you will have created a situation in which the credibility of the system is threatened. You will need to know why line managers are unwilling: do they feel threatened themselves by the new system? (Remember, it highlights their skills, or lack of them.) Do they see it as extra workload? (They will need initial briefing to overcome this, as well as detailed training and development.)

You will need to explore and overcome these initial barriers to effective operation of your assessment system.

You may try a pilot programme to begin with. In this way you can choose your pilot group and make use of those people with the commitment and drive to help you make the system work. People usually feel less threatened, and put up fewer barriers, when they see a system actually operating, and operating well. Plan your pilot carefully and make sure everyone knows what is going on.

Training of Assessors

This is vital. Assessors are no different from anyone else. Would you take on new operatives, or new managers without providing training? (Some organizations may answer yes to this!)

Everyone needs to learn what the expectations of a role are. They need to understand the importance of the role activity and the procedures which need to be followed. Assessors need to understand several aspects of the competence-based system:

- principles of competence-based assessment;
- what makes it different from other forms of assessment;
- using standards of competence;
- rules of assessment;
- rules of evidence;
- methods of assessment;
- room for flexibility and creativity;
- roles of assessors and individuals;
- the quality-assurance structure in which the assessment system operates;
- benefits of the assessment system.

You should ensure that a training programme is provided for assessors immediately before the system is put into operation. Selected assessors should be briefed prior to the formal training, so that they can prepare their staff and deal with any concerns which may arise.

Assessors will also need follow-up support. You should consider establishing 'assessor networks' – opportunities for assessors to meet and discuss concerns, difficulties and successes. All of this activity contributes to the quality of the assessment system and encourages commitment and involvement. The network activity also provides an opportunity for assessors to discuss and identify any common training needs which may arise, such as feedback skills, coaching, further training in assessment methods, interpersonal skills and so on.

Monitoring of Assessors

The process of monitoring assessment is usually called *verification*. Your competence-based assessment system should operate within a verification framework. The extent of this framework will depend upon the extent of your system. For example, an in-house system leading to company certification of individual performance might have a three-tier

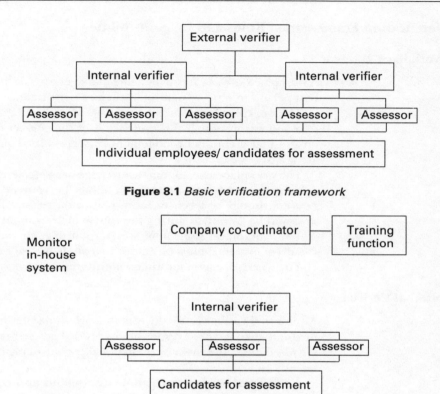

Figure 8.1 *Basic verification framework*

Figure 8.2 *Verification framework for in-company model of competence-based assessment*

system, whereas one linked to national certification would have as many as seven tiers. Figure 8.1 illustrates a basic verification framework. A model for an in-company system is illustrated in Figure 8.2.

Each assessor needs to be monitored to ensure reliability of assessment – that is, that the same judgement would be reached by more than one assessor when the same collection of evidence of competence is assessed.

To achieve this, you will need someone who monitors the assessors (an internal verifier) and a central coordinator.

The remainder of this chapter outlines the responsibilities of these key roles and other quality-assurance procedures which can be applied at national and at corporate or departmental level.

Verification Frameworks: Roles and Responsibilities

Workplace Assessor

A workplace assessor is usually a line manager, since a line manager is the best person to observe natural workplace performance.

The workplace assessor is responsible for collecting *evidence of performance* and ensuring that this evidence is of the correct *type* and *quality* to ensure that a confident judgement of success in required standards is achieved.

The workplace assessor may use a range of assessment methods but the primary form of assessment must always be *observation of performance*. *Feedback* should be given to individuals on a regular basis and *training needs* will be identified during the course of assessment.

The workplace assessor is also responsible for *recording assessment*. Details of evidence must be entered on an *assessment record*.

The workplace assessor will be monitored by an *internal verifier*.

Internal Verifier

An internal verifier is usually someone who operates in-company at the next line-management responsibility level. The verifier's role is to oversee assessment and make sure that quality-control procedures are maintained.

An internal verifier will sample assessments and countersign assessment records. He or she is monitored by an *external verifier* (or company coordinator).

External Verifier

An external verifier is usually an employee of an awarding body or institution and visits the assessment sites on a regular basis.

The external verifier will wish to see individuals' records of assessment and may also sample evidence collected. He or she will check that quality-control systems are fully operational and will report back to the awarding body or institution on any difficulties encountered.

The external verifier, appointed by the national awarding body (or the company coordinator in an in-company system), has responsibility for monitoring the overall assessment process and for passing on recommendations for certification to the awarding-body management structure. This is where a possible seven-tier system comes into play (see Figure 8.3).

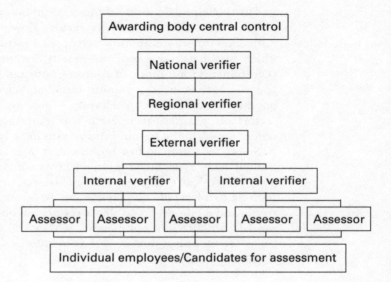

Figure 8.3 *Extended verification framework*

Approval of Assessment Sites

If your organization operates within a national assessment system, it is likely that you will be required to go through an approval process for each site at which you wish to operate assessment.

If you operate your own in-company system, you will still want to ensure that a common system operates at all locations or in all subsidiaries. The following guidelines on the approval and monitoring processes which operate within the UK system at national level can therefore be applied at corporate level by substituting 'corporate body' for 'awarding body' and 'subsidiary' for 'assessment centre'.

The approval process usually requires the payment of a registration fee after certain aspects relating to operation of the assessment have been checked against criteria set by the awarding body. These include:

- trained assessors;
- use of approved recording systems;
- internal monitoring (verification).

As the awarding bodies have to recoup their own quality-monitoring costs, they often make a charge for registration of assessment centres and for materials, the latter being centrally devised.

This is helpful in establishing a common system across all occupational roles within an industry sector. However, it does cause some difficulties for organizations which operate within several sectors, each of which may have their own assessment documentation and their own requirements for training of assessors. For example, in your organization you may have managers, administration and clerical staff and those who operate in various technical roles – at least three or four 'industry sectors'. If you have to operate a different assessment and recording system for each, the training and resourcing costs start to look ominous!

Some awarding bodies require that your appointed assessors are trained using a specific programme. This actually goes against the grain: a key principle of competence-based assessment and qualifications is that training to a level of competence should be available by a wide range of routes and methods. To say that assessors can only be deemed acceptable (and by implication, competent) if they are trained by one route is therefore stepping outside the principles in which the system itself should be operating.

Procedures for Certification

Once again, if you are introducing a nationally recognized system, the procedures for certification will be included (or should be) in the initial briefing materials provided by the awarding body(ies).

This usually includes procedures by which the record of assessment – which may be a logbook provided by the awarding body – is signed by the assessor and countersigned by the internal verifier once sufficient evidence of competence has been collected. The record will then continue through the quality-assurance framework to the external verifier and thence to the central office of the awarding body where computer records will be updated and certificates issued.

Certificates can be issued on a unit-by-unit basis as well as a full qualification (ie, a required number of units). In a company certification scheme, where the corporate body would be the awarding body, a similar set of procedures would need to be established. A computerized database to store records of achievement and issue of certificates would be essential where large numbers of unit-based certificates were awarded.

► REVIEW ◄

This chapter has briefly outlined the key quality-assurance issues within a competence-based assessment system. Further guidance can be found in the References and Further Reading.

References and Further Reading

Bill, L. (1990) 'The Comparability of Examination Systems and Certificates used in the Various Countries of Europe.' Paper to the 16th International Conference, Maastricht, International Association for Educational Assessment, June 1990.

Bourke, J B, Hansen, J H, Houston, W R and Johnson C. (1975) *Criteria for Describing and Assessing Competency Programmes*, Syracuse University, NY, National Consortium of Competency Based Education Centers.

Boyatzis, R E (1982) *The Competent Manager*, Wiley, New York.

Burke, J W (Ed) (1989) *Competency Based Education and Training*, Falmer Press, London.

Elam, S (1971) *Performance Based Teacher Education: What is the State of the Art?*, American Association of Colleges of Teacher Education, Washington DC.

Fletcher, S (1991a) *Designing Competence-based Training*, Practical Trainer Series, Kogan Page, London, and Pfeiffer & Co, San Diego.

Fletcher, S (1991b) *NVQs, Standards and Competence: A Practical Guide for Employers, Managers and Trainers*. Kogan Page in association with Godfrey Durham Training Consultants Ltd, London.

HMSO, (1986) *A Review of Vocational Qualifications in England and Wales: Final Report*, Manpower Services Commission, National Economic Development Office, London.

Management Charter Initiative (1991) *Implementation Pack*, MCI, London.

Mansfield, B and Matthews, D (1985) *Job Competence: A Description for use in Vocational Education and Training*, FESC/ESF Core Skills Project, Bristol.

Mitchell, L (1989) 'The Definition of Standards & their Assessment', in Burke, *op cit*.

MSC, (1981) *A New Training Initiative: Agenda for Action*, Manpower Services Commission, Sheffield.

NCVQ (1991) *Criteria and Related Guidance*, NCVQ, London.

Swanchek and Campbell (1981) 'Competence/performance-based Teacher Education: the Unfulfilled Promise', *Educational Technology* June, pp 5–10.

Training Agency (1988–90) *The Development of Assessable Standards of Occupational Competence*, Standards Methodology Unit, Moorfoot, Sheffield.

Training Agency (1989) *Development of Assessable Standards for National Certification: Guidance Notes*, Training Agency, Sheffield.

Training Agency (1990) *Competence and Assessment*, issues 6–12 and special editions, Training Agency, Sheffield.